TWO PATHS TO GOD

Fintan Creaven SJ

Two Paths to God

the columba press

First published in 2012 by
the columba press
55A Spruce Avenue, Stillorgan Industrial Park,
Blackrock, Co. Dublin

Cover by Bill Bolger
Origination by The Columba Press
Printed by MPG Books Limited

ISBN 978-1-85607-793-4

Contents

Introduction

There are two strong threads of spirituality at work in me, one derived from an affinity with the early Celtic Church and the other with the spirituality of Ignatius of Loyola and the Jesuits. Having family connections with Ireland and having spent over ten years working in Scotland as a Jesuit, I have found a strong affinity with the Celtic mentality and the spirituality of the early Celtic Christian Church. Aligned with this, there is a strong vein of spirituality in me derived from my life as a Jesuit.

As time has gone on I have speculated as to what it would be like to bring the two threads together and see whether there are common elements in them. I was beginning to think I was on a wild goose chase when I discovered *Celtic Threads*, a book edited by Padraigin Clancy. There is a reference in this book to a form of retreat used in Ireland, called 'Siol' Retreat, described by Fionnuala Ni Chuill. She had discovered that Celtic and Ignatian spiritualities shared a common core, and they blended together easily. This has encouraged me, in this book, to explore more deeply, both of these paths to God. Doing so, I am sure, can be beneficial, helping the reader to reflect on his or her own spiritual life of prayer.

Of course, it hardly needs saying that the two paths cannot be exactly parallel since they are separated by over eight hundred years and each has been influenced by its own social background and ecclesiastical structure. Ignatius lived in a post-Reformation era when the Roman Church was being challenged by the reformers. The Inquisition flourished at that time and Ignatius was closely questioned by it on more than one occasion. The structure of the early Christian Church was not on the Roman model until well after the Synod of Whitby, AD 664, and was based on a model derived from monastic life. Their bishops were usually part of a monastic community. But even given the differences imposed by time and culture there is much to be gained by juxtaposing the two paths.

Wisdom is timeless as is spirituality, and although their expression may vary and change over time, the truths they express do not change. We still find help and solace from the psalms and the Old Testament prophets and the writings of the saints from the time of Christ up to the present day.

In its early years the Celtic culture was largely oral. Alexander Carmichael discovered this as he walked through the Hebridean islands gathering the prayers and runes of the Celtic people there. Despite all the religious changes that had taken place on these islands he found that the old people could remember the prayers that they had learned years before when they were children. From what he discovered and from other sources such as manuscripts we can get a sense of the spirituality of the people.

The essence of Ignatian spirituality can be gleaned especially from the *Spiritual Exercises* which Ignatius wrote down, and continually amended, during his own spiritual conversion and journey. Since these *Exercises* are referred to frequently in the text of this book, I think it would be beneficial to outline the structure and contents of them here.

The *Spiritual Exercises*, although written down by Ignatius, are not intended to be used by reading them, but by praying and experiencing them. They can be called a scheme of prayer and meditative reflection largely derived from scripture and prefaced by a series of twenty notes (referred to as Annotations), intended as helps for both the person giving the *Exercises* and the one receiving them (whom I shall call the 'Pilgrim'). The Fourth Annotation indicates the structure of the whole: there are four 'weeks' or sections of the *Exercises*. The word 'week' does not mean a calendar week but a length of several days.

Preceding these weeks there is a Presupposition and what is called the 'First Principle and Foundation'. The Presupposition is aimed at the giver of the *Exercises*, asking him or her to put the best construction possible on any statement of the pilgrim.

The 'First Principle and Foundation' is proposed as a basic foundation and point of reference of the whole spiritual edifice of the *Exercises* and something for the pilgrim to consider and ruminate upon as the *Exercises* start. Although the statement is proposed in terms which sound rather dry and academic they are to be prayed about in an affective atmosphere of generosity and openness to God's Spirit. It proposes that our purpose in life is 'to praise, reverence and serve God and so save our souls'.

This rather strong emphasis on personal salvation gives way, as the *Exercises* proceed, to praise of God and his glory.

The First Week itself consists of five meditations, leading through what we might call a 'history of sin' and its nature, to our own sin and sinfulness, but leading to a deep realisation of God's love and forgiveness.

The Second, and longest, Week moves the pilgrim into a dwelling upon the call of the King and the life of Christ as experienced in a series of 'imaginative' contemplations of the events of the gospels. In the process, the pilgrim moves closer to the Person of Christ and into a desire to follow him. This may involve a decision by the pilgrim to alter his or her way of life so as to give better expression to the following of Christ in a practical mode of living and working.

The Third Week is given over to following through the Passion of Christ. If the pilgrim really wishes to follow Christ, then it will involve being with him in his Passion and suffering.

Finally, in the Fourth Week the pilgrim finds joy and praise as he or she contemplates the Risen Lord. As part of this week there is a prayer called the *Contemplation* to deepen the love of God in us, leading to finding God present in the whole of our world and in everything we do and experience.

By following this scheme the pilgrim moves into a deeper giving of his or her life to Christ and his Father.

CHAPTER ONE

The Triune Source

Thee, God, I come from, to Thee go
All day I like fountain flow
From thy hand out, swayed about
Mote-like in thy mighty glow
(Gerard Manley Hopkins, *Thee, God, I Come From*)

Jesus spoke in many beautiful parables and stories of the reign of God. But when he came to speak of the nature of God his words had that ring of personal experience that commands our attention. That experience was the Trinity.

It has been said that if silence could be a heresy then the silence of many Christians concerning the Trinity would constitute heresy! Millions of our fellow human beings have no sense of the Trinity even if they do pray to 'God'.

Personal prayer is directed, generally speaking, to the person of Christ, or the Holy Spirit, or Mary, or one of the saints, or just 'God'.

Yet a firm belief in God as Trinity was one of the strongest tenets of the Christianity of the early Celts. It is expressed over and over again in their prayers:

God is an all-powerful yet kindly Father,
Jesus, the Son, is a man of tears and sorrow,
And the Holy Spirit is their helper.

And the prayer goes on to ask for cleansing and protection and sanctification. God is also seen as king of the elements at the helm of our boat, leading us peacefully to the end of our journey.

It might be easy enough to imagine Patrick standing on a knoll, talking to a small group of Celtic people, the breeze blowing his hair as he held up a sprig of shamrock, turning left and right so that the group could see such a small plant. They stared at him, gripped by what he was saying.

It would be easy to imagine it, but unfortunately we know that in fact the shamrock did not take its place as an image of the Trinity until some years after the time of Patrick. Be that as it may, this man had a great influence in organising the Christian faith for the Celtic peoples of Ireland. A fundamental element of that faith was a belief in a God who was three; Father, Son and Spirit. This faith in the Triune God came into Ireland well before the time of Patrick and was already present in the faith of the Christians in Britain.

Patrick was used to walking, praying and weaving words in the open country, he who had been a slave, a sheep-minder in the fields and on the hills. It was on the fells that he had met God in prayer and praying and worshipping in the open air was habitual to the Christian Celts.

The idea of a Triune God, creator and source of all being, was not totally foreign to the listeners. The druids were familiar with the threesomeness of gods and goddesses. So, when Patrick preached a Triune God to them they could accept it without stress. The Trinitarian vision of God entered naturally into their consciousness and imagination. The great prayer attributed to Patrick, *St Patrick's Breastplate*, invokes the Trinity straightaway: 'I bind to myself today the strong name of the Trinity, the Three in one and One in three.' However, the prayer in its present form is much later than Patrick.

The particular belief in the Trinity came from the gospel of St John, the most loved and used gospel for the Celtic Christian Church. Its quality of contemplative beauty held their imaginative souls in thrall, supporting their faith. It was John who recounted the conversation of Jesus in which he described his relationship to the Father and the Spirit. 'You must believe me when I say that I am in the Father, and the Father is in me ... The Advocate, the Holy Spirit, whom the Father will send in my name, will teach you everything.'

Their love of the three-fold God grew into a national faith. They have been described as a people intoxicated by God, to the extent that every aspect of their lives was privy to his presence. God was both the Transcendent Being, above and beyond everything, untouchable, unfindable, in fact, un-everything you could possibly describe with mere human words; but paradoxically, he was also immanently present within every aspect of creation. Anywhere you look, there is God present. He is in all things, the wind, the sea, the clouds, the hills, the living things

... all were home to this most homely God. St Patrick, pressed by a questioner to describe his God said:

Our God is a God of all people,
A God of heaven and of earth and all that is in it, seas and rivers,
A God of the sun and moon and stars, God of high mountains and valleys.
He is above, and under and in heaven, he dwells there and in the earth and sea and in everything that is in the earth and sea.
He inspires all things, he quickens all things, supports all things, is over all things, inspiring, quickening all. He makes the sun to shine and surrounds the moon and stars.
He puts wells in the dry earth, places dry islands in the sea.

So, for the Celt reading the *Exercises of Ignatius* for the first time there would be no trouble in understanding the prayer called the *Contamplatio ad amorem (Contemplation for Love)* in the Fourth Week of the *Exercises*:

To look how God dwells in creatures, in the elements giving them being, in the plants vegetating, in the animals feeling in them, in us, giving us understanding; and in me, giving me being, life, senses and mind. God is present in all creation. Look to your left, he is there, look to your right, he is there, look up, look down, he is there.

The Celts were a naturally religious people. They were used to God and saw spirits in nature and in all the events of life. Their prayers were shaped to the event, asking the Trinity to be present. If ever you had doubts about the Trinitarian belief of the Celtic Christian Church you need only look at their prayers. There are many examples of the prayers cast in a Trinitarian form:

Today I will walk with the Father,
Today I will walk with Christ,
Today I will walk with the Spirit,
Triune and all loving.

It is not so much inviting the Trinity to be present as assuming his kindly and loving presence. God *is* present in all things whether we invite him or not. If we want to compose prayers for an event, this form involving Father, Son and Spirit is very useful. Even in their sleep they knew the presence of God:

> God with me tonight as I lie down,
> Christ with me tonight as I lie down,
> Spirit with me tonight as I lie down;
> God, Christ, and Spirit lie down with me.

The Triune God was part and parcel of their lives. There are prayers for the night and the morning, for washing, for cooking, for smooring the fire in the evening and rekindling it next morning, for milking the cows and making the butter. Time and time again these prayers were Trinitarian.

> Today I come to the Father,
> Today I come to the Son,
> Today I come to the powerful Spirit;
> With God I come this day,
> With Christ I come this day,
> With the soothing Spirit I come.

Their prayers show how deep was their sense of God's presence and how pervasive was the action of the Trinity in their lives. Many of the Celtic saints had mystical experiences of the presence of God or of the saints. The Trinity was an everyday experience for them. It was not a dogma in the realm of ideas but a lived experience that was rooted strongly within them.

It had an equally strong root in the belief of St Ignatius. Living as he did in the 16th century under the influence of Catholic Spain (though he himself was Basque) he would have been brought up in a strongly religious atmosphere. His religion was part of his upbringing though he did not live it fully until later in life. The great artists of the time were representing religious subjects as a normal part of their output. El Greco painted a picture of the Trinity in 1577. Even in the later conflicts of the Reformation, the Trinity was not impugned.

Alongside the articles of faith that Ignatius was fed in his childhood and youth was a life lived without any deep commitment to them, the life of a Catholic by name but not by conviction. That is, until the time when he went through that terrible purging of the spirit when he was at Manresa. At that time his long-held, but loosely gripped, articles of faith became deep convictions, held with the living of a new life. I have little doubt that had his Catholic faith been insulted by a sceptic before this 'conversion' he would have defended that faith with his sword, but more, I feel, out of reaction to the insult rather than the love of the faith.

The young chick in the nest suddenly realises that flight is real, and stands wobbling on the edge of the safe place where it was fed until that moment. But now it must jump. Its life, at that point, is suddenly, brutally changed into a commitment.

Ignatius used to pray the office of the church as his spiritual sensitivity grew and took command of his life. Praying the office one day on the steps of the local monastery, he had a powerful experience. He was saying the prayers to each of the Persons of the Trinity and then to the Trinity as a whole when he saw the Trinity represented to him as three notes of a musical instrument, the three notes forming one chord, one harmony. The experience was so strong that it changed his life and perception and he was like a child with a new toy, proclaiming the Trinity all day long, in images and praises which tumbled out of him like a mountain stream cascading out of a cliff face. He joined a procession leaving the monastery, but as he walked he could not stop the crying and sobbing and this continued until dinner time. After dinner he talked and talked about the Trinity, using many illustrations and comparisons, and was obviously full of great joy and consolation.

From that day on, the Trinity was a major part of his prayer and spirituality. You can read the result in his spiritual diary. Time and time again he prayed to the Trinity, he said the Mass of the Trinity, and quite often his prayer brought on great gushes of tears to the extent that he feared for his eyesight. They were not tears of sorrow, but rather of a deep sense of the beauty and truth of the vision. You get the feeling on reading his diary that he had instant access to the presence of the Trinity. He describes at least fifteen occasions when he had a perception of the Trinity while saying or preparing to celebrate Mass. In 1544, he said the Mass of the Trinity many times. On Tuesday, 19 February of that year, for instance, during Mass he had many intuitions of the

Trinity which led to an enlightenment of his understanding. He commented that this enlightenment could not have been gained even with long and hard study. Again, on 21 February, he writes:

> During Mass I knew or had a feeling, or a vision (God knows which!) that I was speaking to the Father and seeing that he was One Person of the Blessed Trinity, I felt moved to love all the Trinity, especially as the other Persons were all in the Trinity by their very essence etc.

It was this insistence that he could not have had such intuitions of the Trinity by studying, even for a lifetime, that shows the power of his sense of the presence of the Triune God to him. The Trinity seemed to bestow on him a participation in its life, calling him to the very depths of the Spirit. The Mass seemed to be the entry point for his awareness of the Trinity with the consequent bringing on of floods of tears. Sometimes he saw one Person of the three, at others he saw all three. At times his vision depicts Jesus as guide and companion, but without losing the sense of being in the presence of the whole Trinity.

The experience for him was both intellectual and affective. Although his mind became enlightened, it was not simply an intellectual experience, but his affective self was deeply moved. There were never any 'nuptial' images such as are found in other great mystics. He mentions the Church as the Bride of Christ, but never the individual soul in that way. Instead, his mysticism is one of service, giving rise to the phrase, 'Contemplatives in Action' as a description of his Jesuit followers.

This uniting of the mystical and practical can be seen in both Celtic and Ignatian experience. The Celtic approach to reality held together the deeply mystical and the profoundly practical. They were seen as two sides of the same coin. For the Celt, the Trinity is an experience to be lived, rather than a philosophical and speculative (or even mathematical!) conundrum to be pondered and argued about, which it tended to be in Western theology. The Celts leaned more to the East than the West in their theology and spirituality. The Cappadocians saw and experienced the Trinity as relational and community building.

The group that gathered around Ignatius and who became the first Jesuits, formed a community around their leader and with Christ. The Trinity is a divine community centred in self-giving love. It comes, then, as a surprise that the Trinity is often more assumed than actually named in the pages of the *Spiritual Exercises*. God is present there, the Creator, the Lord and for Ignatius everything comes down from above *de arriba* and everything must return that way. We are drawn to God, who is the instress of our being. I recall visiting a man who had a dog. We sat in the lounge until the host got up to go to the kitchen to make us a cup of tea. He left the dog in the lounge and closed the door. Though I tried talking to the dog, patting its head and scratching its ears, it sat resolutely facing the door in wrapt awareness of what was happening in the kitchen. At the slightest sound from there, the rattle of a cup and saucer, the turning on of a tap, the ears of the dog would lift. Its whole being was turned towards its master. As I watched it I wished I could be as attentive to God in my prayers!

> To You I lift up my eyes, You who dwell in the heavens;
> My eyes like the eyes of slaves on the hand of their Lord,
> … like the eyes of a servant on the hand of her mistress.
> (Ps 122)

One clear reference to the Triune Source is found at the beginning of the Second Week of the *Spiritual Exercises* where Ignatius asks the person doing the retreat to contemplate how the Divine Persons were gazing down on the earth and its people rushing down to hell; and the decision was taken that the Second Person was to become human to save the peoples of the earth. So the mystery of the incarnation was set in motion.

There is a wonderful poem of R. S. Thomas (called 'The Coming') in which the Father is pointing out the round ball of the world to his Son, with its people crying out for help; and the poem ends with the Son pleading: 'Let me go there, Father!' It shows the desire of the Son (and therefore of the whole Trinity) to come to our earth, and become one of us. St Paul expresses this in the letter to the Philippians: 'Though his essence was divine he did not cling to his Godhead but emptied himself to become one of us.'

The Trinity was at the heart of Celtic spirituality. It was more a vision and an experience for them than a dogma. They were influenced by the East rather than the West in their theology and the Trinity was seen as a relational reality. At the heart of the Godhead are relationships of self-giving love. Love is constantly on the move in the Godhead, the one moving towards and into the other as shown so powerfully in the Trinity Icon of Rublev. Each faces towards another. The lovely Greek word, *Perichoresis* expressed for them the interpenetration of the Persons, different persons united – diversity in unity and unity in diversity. The image that immediately jumps into mind is that of a dance. Who said that God does not move?

We are created in the image of the Trinity, and so, stamped into our being is the need for community, for interconnectedness. We are in relationships of various sorts in our lives, relationships reflecting this image of the Trinity. We are in relationship with God, with each other, with the earth, and within ourselves. Being 'children of the earth' in Rahner's phrase, our relationship with God is expressed in our love for one another, our care for the earth, and our knowledge of ourselves and what is most for our good. That does not mean that we don't need special times of intimacy with God in our prayer and reflective life. Praying to the Trinity – rather neglected these days – helps us to get in touch with the truths expressed in John's gospel in chapters 14 and 15 in which Jesus is telling us about his relationship to the Father and how he is 'the Way to the Father'. Our prayer life is of prime importance in our spiritual existence, renewing, as it does, our spiritual energy for our daily contact with the world of our work and relationships.

In the Christian faith our relationships with each other are like a great corridor that we walk along in the house of God. The way in which those relationships are lived and expressed exhibit our movement towards God. If they are leading us away from God we are in the wrong corridor, even in the wrong house!

Nowadays, the relationship to the earth is more recognised as being a God-given command to care for creation. More and more we are seeing the need for this as we become aware of our disregard for the life of creation on the one hand, and slaughtering of it on the other.

Our relationship to ourselves acts like an internal reflector that keeps us in contact with the right road.

These various relationships are our living out of that image of the Trinity within us.

In the dark abysses of the sea below,
impenetrable to our sight,
a wonderful, mesmeric, mind-entrancing world
exists, so deep we cannot see.
Above, beyond our world-embracing air,
out in the vast incalculable space,
there breathes a vast, tumultuous, majestic,
unimaginably live and active
Universe,
exploding outwards, at a fearful rate,
totally beyond our sight or mind.
The things we cannot see
are yet so real, so living!
But below, above, beyond, all these,
away among the trillion-folds of stars,
there lives a Presence so immensely Huge
we cannot even think of it.
The Triune God IS.
Why Three?
Only the breathing of One to Another,
the In-Othering kenotic life of Three,
can express for us the one word we can
truly say: and that is Love.

CHAPTER TWO

The Other World

'There are two worlds, the visible and the invisible as the Creed speaks ("Maker ... of all things visible and invisible"). The world we do not see really exists though we do not see it, and this other world is quite as great and quite as close to us as the one we do see.' So said Cardinal Newman in a sermon. He says that this other world that we do not see is more wonderful and all around us. Only faith can see it. Newman's sermon would have been no news to the early Celtic Christians.

Were we to imagine an ancient Celtic Christian finding a copy of the *Spiritual Exercises of St Ignatius Loyola*, in a form which he or she could read, we might wonder whether there would be anything familiar in it? Different modes of expression and ideas there would be, and different cultural attitudes, but there would also be a familiar belief structure. I could imagine the avid reader turning page after page and seeing framed there, in words and thoughts, the shapes and dreams that measure his or her own heart and soul. 'I *know* that – *Yes!*' and the book might become a sacred source.

But perhaps not! The *Spiritual Exercises* is not a book of ideas but a practical methodology for approaching God, the same God for both the Celtic and Ignatian seeker.

Over all, there would be a deep sense of the being and presence of God. In fact, throughout the document there would be a stress on awareness, a desire to move into that Presence more fully. The Celtic Christians were a people wrapped in God, a possession which determined their lives and understanding.

Their God was not a distant, unapproachable deity, hidden behind the clouds of their understanding, but a God immediately present to them ('immanent' as we would say), a God that invaded, or rather pre-empted, everything they thought and did. They lived in a glad and life-giving atmosphere of God-presence. As St Patrick once put it, God is in everything. So, for the Celt, reading the *Exercises* of Ignatius for the first time, there would be no trouble in understanding the prayer that we saw in the last chapter, how God dwells in the elements, creatures, plants and animals of this earth. God is present in all creation.

Ignatius of Loyola traces steps for us to come into the presence of this God more and more fully in the *Spiritual Exercises*. He wrote these exercises as a result of his own experience. And his own day-dreaming! It could be said that his 'conversion' to a God-gripped life was the result of this day-dreaming. As he lay on his bed of recuperation, after a cannonball had shattered his leg, he indulged in imagining his battles with the Saracens, and the jousts in which he would impress a fair lady (of very high rank – a hopeless quest!).

It was when he started to read the only books available in his pious brother's house, the gospels and the lives of the saints (*Flos Sanctorum*), that his perception began to shift. He began to get a taste for this new reading. New desires and hopes appeared on his horizon, leading eventually to a change in his whole life, in his mindset, his desires, intentions and actions. It was a mind-blowing, or perhaps a soul-blowing, change towards God. Is that so strange? Our imagining reveals our deepest desires. Like an ancient Celtic Christian, his life became God-centred.

It has been said that we relate to the world around us by an inner light – that of perception. It has even been said that this light of perception creates the world around us. But by the further light of imagination we can find access to what Kathleen Raine called the Celtic sense of the 'Mountain behind the mountain'. The Celts had an intense sense of the presence of God in all things. This awareness extended beyond the physical and material realm to embrace a spiritual world. It was that awareness which was expressed in the phrase 'Mountain behind the mountain'. The Celt looking at the mountain would see not just the physical reality, the rocks and grassy slopes, but also 'see' the whole invisible world behind that mountain.

Mountain behind the mountain: an ordinary mountain, very physical, material, peat bogs, streams, earth, air, fire, water, sun, moon, wind and rain. But also, a place of presence and presences. Those who can 'see' will know the mountain behind the mountain. It is a primal perception with which we 'see' the world of spirits and the presence of God. This sort of seeing involves a form of imagination. With primal perception we 'see' the world of spirits and the presence of God. Seeing this involves a form of imagination.

A sense of presence may invade us, a moment of transcendence, a realisation that there is more here than just the rocks and grass and flowers. It is imbued with a spiritual being. A person who walks on that mountain and who has an imaginative sense will be aware of that presence. *How* do I know this other world? Not, certainly, by scientific experiment and observation. It is not subject to measurement and analysis. It can be 'seen' only by the person with insight, imagination and faith. A person who comes to you and expresses an experience of the presence of God is trying to say something which cannot be compassed by words.

The Celts had a strong sense of presence. They were a God-captured people. Their lives were embraced on all sides by the Divine Being. It was an experience of the immanent God, rather than the transcendent God. Transcendence can result in the division between religion and nature, and that was not the Celtic way of thinking or experiencing. God for them was everywhere present. The immanent God comes from a deep sense and understanding of the incarnation.

The Celtic awareness of God in all things extended beyond the physical and material realm to embrace also the spirit world. A narrow line, a thin veil, divided this world from the other. There were some 'entry points' such as cemeteries, which were considered to be ways into the other world.

They were a people with a gift of bringing together the spiritual and material worlds, seeing one in and through the other. They did not spend time searching for the division between the two, looking for where the secular ended and the spiritual began. The thinness of the veil gave a strong sense of the closeness and proximity of the dead. Life beyond death was very real for them. 'Seeing as we are compassed about with so great a cloud of witnesses.' (Heb 12:1) They had an almost physical sense of the company of heaven around God, saints, angels and other heavenly powers. 'When we raise our eyes to heaven we raise them to a great host, for God is the Lord of Hosts.'

St Columbanus shows in his sermons that deep sense of the other world of spiritual realities. Like Newman, he saw this world, our visible world, as less real than the invisible one. What, I ask, is the difference between what I saw yesterday and the dream I had this night? Do they not seem to you today to be equally unreal?

This sense of a real but invisible world is one which enlivens their whole outlook on life. A person who walks the earth surrounded by the presence of a cloud of witnesses, those beings of the Spirit world, cannot but be affected by them. Although we cannot 'see' with our bodily eyes this 'other world' of spiritual reality, nevertheless it would be rash to think that we are untouched and unaffected by it. It is only by allowing the realisation of that world that we can become fully human. To ignore it, or refuse to see it, results in the sad condition that our world and its people are in. Suppressing the possibility of the spiritual world results in a grossly materialistic outlook on life, with the consequent forms of idolatry and distortion that are so common in our time. On the other hand, the awareness of it prevents us from rooting like pigs for truffles in a rank earthly materialism. To be aware of the possibility of the other world even though it is unseen, gives us a wider vision and a more fulfilled life.

This spring I watched daffodils appearing and blooming in great glowing bunches in the grounds of the retreat house that I work in. They appear at the appropriate time from the roots in the earth. If the roots stayed as they were in the earth and did not grow into the light, we would never see the beautiful flowers. We are like the root: if we refuse to acknowledge the air and the sky above us and the light we would never flower. Our true greatness, in God's image, would never be fully realised. That is the misfortune of the materialist – he remains in the earth and never acknowledges the spiritual possibilities within him.

Fortunately, we bear the energy of God in us that will enable our earth-root to grow and flower. The importance of our being rooted in the earth is obvious enough. We are 'children of the earth' as Rahner proclaims. But we are also children of the Spirit. We are like a child that bears the genes inherited from its parents and willy-nilly will grow according to that genome, unless he or she deliberately moves in a different direction. We bear the kiss of God in us, the stamp that labels us and directs us to our destination in God.

We are in a time of scientific rationalisation which has lost this way of seeing. To get a sense of the spiritual world requires a wise simplicity and willingness to accept the validity of such a thing as a Spiritual World.

These manifestations of the presence of the other world reality were always, for the Celts, mediated through some finite this-worldly-reality. Their spirituality was down-to-earth, expressed in their prayers which cover daily events, from the rising to the setting of the sun. Their sense of the importance of the little things of life reflected their history of being a little people, often oppressed and marginalised. These prayers for each daily activity acted like a sort of frame on a painting to bring out its beauty. This was the task of ritual and ceremony investing the simplest and most commonplace tasks and events with a sense of worth and a measure of transcendence. We need to reinvest the ordinary, everyday, with a measure of sanctity. God is in the trivial round (because it is not trivial!). The Celts felt the angels with them in their work. Angels and saints are called upon to be present in their tasks:

> May all the saints surround you,
> May all the angels surround you,
> May all the saints and the nine angels be with you.

Noel O'Donoghue writes of this 'other world' in his book *The Mountain Behind the Mountain* (title taken from a poem of Kathleen Raine). Speaking of the importance of imagination he distinguishes between imaginary and imaginal. Imaginary refers to a product of the imagination without any objective reality, works such as the Harry Potter stories. Imaginal refers to the use of imagination to 'visualise' a world that is real but cannot be seen with our physical eyes. We 'see' with the powers of the imagination, a world that is real even though it cannot be seen. This imaginal world is familiar territory in the Bible. The appearance of messengers from that other world is such as to cause awesome fear, but there is no surprise that it happens or what it is. Such appearances are recorded with the assumption that they will be understood and accepted by the reader. No one reading the Old or New Testament can be unaware of the world of spirits and angels, the powers and denominations that St Paul refers to. When the Celtic biographers wrote about people like Columba being surrounded by angels they were doing no more and no less than the Bible writers had been doing. It is no surprise that deep awareness of that other world is a gift that is common to Christians at all times. It is a significant part of the belief system of the early Celtic Christians, fitting in, as it did, to their long-held attitude to creation. The appearance of the three men in white to Abraham, the angel come to talk to Gideon, the companion of Tobias on his journey who turned out to be an angel and many other examples in the Old Testament, all bespeak an awareness of the presence of the other world of spiritual reality. In the New Testament the appearance of angels is often associated with the events of a divine nature in which God is directly involved with the world. Gabriel appears to Mary, a host of them appear to the shepherds; and later at the end of the life of Jesus they are present in the Garden of Gethsemane, in the tomb announcing his resurrection. Many other signs of the other world are present in the Gospels, such as the voice from heaven saying 'This is my Son the Beloved ...' and the transcendent manifestation at the transfiguration. Both Ignatius and the Celtic Christians were brought up with the gospels. Ignatius was given a book of the gospels when his pious brother could find no light reading of a romantic nature to pass away the tiresome hours of recuperation. The appearance of angels and other denizens of heaven are described with regularity in the annals of the Celtic saints. St Columba on Iona was seen to be visited by angels on a little hill known to this day as the Hill of the Angels.

The *Spiritual Exercises* were written in a context of a belief in that other world and by a person whose upbringing and conversion to a dedicated life was immersed in that other world. The visions he had gave witness to his belief. As he recovered from his wounds in the house of his brother he had a vision of Our Lady and the Child which helped him in his struggle against sexual thoughts. Later he had visions of Christ present in the eucharistic host, and of God creating the world. He declared that these visions 'strengthened him'. He never expected that any person wanting to do the *Spiritual Exercises* should be a visionary but I would maintain that a belief in the possibility of a world of a spiritual nature and a belief in God would be expected if a person were to gain the full benefit of the *Exercises*. Yet his style in the *Exercises* is very practical, even pedestrian.

There are those who maintain that the *Spiritual Exercises* are available to anyone of whatever colour of opinion and whatever shade of faith, even for those with no shade of spirituality at all or belief of any kind. But it is difficult to see how a person with no spiritual awareness, and no openness to it, could benefit from a system so immersed in a faith in God and the spiritual king-dom and from a belief in a Christ who is the Son of God. Although any person who stays for thirty days in a place of silent reflection and prayer cannot but benefit from the experi-ence (if he or she really wants to) nevertheless a person without a basic belief structure and contact with a spiritual dimension will find that the *Exercises* speak from a different frame of mind and belief and in a language which is alien to theirs.

Except, perhaps, for the Contemplation in the Fourth Week (*Contemplatio ad amorem*) you would not think of the *Exercises* as a poetic document. His opening note (Annotation 1), for in-stance, is stated in very prosaic, practical terms:

> As strolling, walking and running are bodily exercises, so every way of preparing and disposing the soul to rid itself of all the disordered tendencies, and after it is rid, to seek and find the Divine Will as to the management of one's life for the salvation of the soul, is called Spiritual Exercise.

The *Exercises* provide a practical document for the use of the Christian to go deeper into their life with Christ. The deep awareness of the spiritual world of the early Celtic Christians makes one think that they would have fitted naturally into the mind-frame of Ignatius' *Exercises*. Their spirituality was ex-pressed in very practical ways, as they prayed with arms ex-tended and recited all 150 psalms each day!

The *Spiritual Exercises* often have the effect of a conversion to a deeper spiritual life or even, where appropriate, to a belief in God or Christ and any person entering into these *Exercises* would at least have to have some desire to find a supreme being or hear a call to follow Christ or perhaps just to deepen their spiritual life. One can never, of course, put limits onto what God can do.

From tiny beginnings great things can grow. We think of the Big Bang which set the universe going, a tiny speck exploding to produce everything we can see and speculate about. Again, the tiny seed in the ground can grow to produce a large tree, a great oak or elm. The *Spiritual Exercises* are but a sowing of a seed that sparks a conflagration in the heart, a falling in love if only you can let it grow and nourish it with deep desire.

The *Spiritual Exercises* may work for someone who has not yet come to the realisation or awareness of God and spiritual matters. But there must be some desire for perception. After a deepening realisation of our purpose in life and the centrality of a loving God, the pilgrim is encouraged to ponder on the presence of that God, caught up in his loving embrace. The pilgrim gets to know him as Creator, and Saviour. But even more fundamental, he or she realises that they are made in His image and cannot be fully satisfied or at peace if the God-image in him or her is ignored or suppressed. As Augustine says: 'Thou hast made us for thyself, O God, and our hearts are restless till they rest in thee.'

It could be that a realising of one's sinfulness and need for a better life, will be the spur which opens the person to that awareness and that is part of the structure of Ignatius' scheme. The next section (First Week) is given over to a realisation of our sins and sinfulness but leading on to the joyful knowledge that God still loves us despite our sins, so that we give a sort of whoop of joy and astonishment.

St Patrick, son of a deacon and grandson of a priest, speaks of how he had pulled away from God, not keeping the commandments nor listening to the authority of the Church. Then God enlightened his understanding so that he saw his own need and he could turn back to God. God had mercy on his youthful ignorance. He had a sense that God was looking after him even before that moment of conversion when he gained wisdom.

Ignatius was born into an aristocratic Catholic family, so that the tenets of that faith were familiar to him, yet they bore no power over his life. He lived a superficial and vain life, dominated by fighting and womanising, until, on his bed of recuperation at his brother's home in Loyola, he read the gospels and the lives of the saints which switched his perception into the channel of

God's love and the desire to give his life to God by following Christ.

This sort of thing, this turning of a person's life around, has happened time and again in the annals of Christianity. Augustine of Hippo, picking up a book, read words that changed his whole life. Francis of Assisi heard the words of the gospel read at Mass which encouraged him to give away all he had, including his clothes (!), and follow Christ in poverty. In our own day, stories of conversion to a sense and knowledge of God and the other world is not infrequent. Thomas Merton came gradually to a realisation that the reality of God called for a commitment that was wholehearted. Bede Griffiths also found a God-world beckoning to him.

A spiritual world, then, was common to both the Celtic Christian belief system as it was to the Christians at the time of Ignatius. Much of the *Spiritual Exercises* depends on an imaginative method of prayer using the gospel texts.

A person for whom this was a foreign and unacceptable language would find it difficult to benefit fully from the dynamic of the *Exercises*. But, of course, anything is possible for God!

It is because of this familiarity with the world of God and spirit, a familiarity for both the Celts and Ignatius, that I think our imagined Celt would be standing on the same rockbase as the writer of the *Exercises*, even though there are aspects in which they would differ.

The human being is caught up in longings and desires which often lack resolution. So much of our modern life directs us by advertising towards happiness and fulfilment derived from the things of this earth. As a result the spiritual root in the earth remains unopened. If the grain of wheat remains in the ground it stays unopened. It never blooms into spiritual air, never experiences its time of fulfilment.

I think this would have made a lot of sense to our Celtic seeker exploring the *Exercises*. This Celtic seeker would know of the need for an asceticism with regard to the earthly things that surround them. But they are earthly things given by God and are there for our use and fulfilment. And our enjoyment.

The Principle and Foundation at the beginning of the *Exercises* tells us that we are for God and the things of the earth should be used and experienced in such a way as to lead us to that end which is God. If they do that, we use and enjoy them, if they do not lead us to God, we dispense with them. I think the Celtic Christians would have understood that only too well.

We look back, then, to the Celtic Christians to see a people like fish swimming in a sea which is God. They ate and drank, loved and lived with God. And we look to Ignatius to provide a road with signposts leading in a way that enables us to see how we can come closer to that God, our Creator, Saviour and Lover. The Celts and Ignatius are close together in this.

We are familiar with prayer as a spiritual power, and the miracles of the gospel represent the working of God in our creation. The Church's liturgies reflect this, a sense of joining heavenly and earthly communities and the bringing together of material and spiritual energies. In the First Eucharistic Prayer (the Roman Canon) all the angels and saints are called on by the praying community. This bringing together of the earthly and the heavenly would be quite familiar to the Celtic Christians. The Celtic mind was very practical as well as poetic, and so it would find a warm nest in the *Spiritual Exercises*. Their faith was strongly incarnational with an emphasis on physicality and materiality that supported both asceticism and a strongly sacramental outlook, not to mention sheer human creativity, as we see in Irish art and Welsh poetry of the period.

> Moles of the earth, listen!
> There is a whole bright sky up there
> above the confines of this earthly tunnel
> we live in. Could you but evolve eyes,
> – eyes that can see the Beyond –
> you could enjoy untold happiness.
> Listen, then, to your Mole Prophet
> for he is a Seer.

CHAPTER THREE

Transparent Creation – A Window to God

If you wish to know the Creator you must understand creation, said St Columbanus. Or put in another way: if you wish to meet the Creator you need to appreciate creation; see it, experience it, to fall down, like the poet, Mary Oliver, into the long grass.

This chapter is concerned with creation, that is, with everything created, and particularly with the way in which it was regarded by the Christian Celts and by Ignatius. There is a similarity in the way they saw creation, in the way they held it in great respect as God's work. Many people consider the early Celtic Christians to be 'greens' and when asked what their spirituality means to them they would say that it is a spirituality wedded to creation and the natural world. That is what is so attractive about it for a large number of people today. In fact, it has been claimed that Christianity has been rooted first of all in Greek thinking, then in the authority and law of Rome and then in nature in the Celtic world.

The same claims would probably not be made for St Ignatius. Few would automatically think of him as a nature-lover. More likely they would think of him as an ascetic pragmatist. We don't read of him wandering in the woods reciting poetry and describing twigs in the manner of Gerard Manley Hopkins. Yet a perusal of the sources shows us a man who contemplated the stars at night on the roof of the house in Rome where he was staying and felt quite inspired by doing so. The *Contemplation for Love* in the *Spiritual Exercises* is surely a wonderful testimony to a visionary soul who could see God's eyes shining through the fabric of the world. For that is the nub of the matter for both the Celts and for Ignatius: they both knew a God present in the very texture and life of the earth. Where God is absent the earth is there for exploitation. Where God is recognised to be present there is a call for reverence for all that is created. Even a parched and spare landscape has power to make the beholder aware of his or her inner self, as Kathleen Norris declared when gazing at the landscape of Dakota. It is this reverence which establishes creation as sacred, while the loss of it gives rise to the exploitation that is characteristic of a more profane outlook. Creation is God's work and so is blessed. When God looked at what he had made he found it 'very good'. Hence, we cannot brand it as evil or in any sense outside of God's care. As the Book of Wisdom says: 'Hate and create thou couldst not.'

Mircea Eliade described eloquently the difference between the religious outlook on the world and that of the non-religious person. Nature, for the former, is always instinct with a religious value. The cosmos is a divine creation and hence sacred. This is recognisable in the very structure of the world. As the religious person contemplates the world he or she discovers what Eliade calls the many modalities of the sacred, and thus of being. The sacred quality shines through creation which is transparent to it. This is surely something we would do well to gain from Celtic and Ignatian spiritualities. Being the work of the divine creator, creation is not simply good but is also a window through which we can get a glimpse (even when the glass is frosted!) of God still at work.

This would not have been news to the Celts. The sacred, for them, was an absolute reality, out there beyond what can be seen, yet visible within it to those who are perceptive. It is this sacredness that makes things real. Life itself, coming from this sacred source, finds its fullness only in recognising the source.

Where life's transcendent quality goes unrecognised, reality becomes relative; we then live in a pragmatic wandering. All our actions such as eating and drinking, making love, working or playing, become just bodily functions with no spiritual significance. Reverence for creation is absent, and such a world then becomes a resource for our use, our own comfort and convenience. These become the only norms of worth, without any reference to any outside value beyond that of the human.

The respect for the earth characteristic of the Celtic peoples was by no means confined to them. The native Indians of North America and the Aborigines of Australia had a similar attitude to creation. In the case of the Celts this reverence had pre-Christian roots, celebrated in the songs of the bards who, while they may not have made specific reference to the sacred, were not thereby singing in a purely secular key. Sacred and secular were coterminous.

If nature is regarded as totally separate from God (or indeed if there is no God to be separate from) then there is no reason not to loot it for its goods except, of course, that it will eventually end in the destruction of human life as we know it. Even evolving into grass-eaters won't help if the grass is thick with poison and we cannot breathe the air! We need a renewal of respect for nature as God's work which both the Celts and Ignatius upheld as part of their spirituality. Landscapes, says Barry Lopez, are crucibles of mystery, alive and containing all other life, and not to be improved by technology. Our society has pushed God into the background and left us to dominate nature and we need to recover our true position in the world.

Although nature is imbued with the life of God, it is transparent only to the contemplative eye and heart. Certain aspects of God become apparent to the sensitive eye. The joy of God in his creation is communicated in our own joy at the presence of the life of the wilds, often conveyed by poets:

> Nothing is so beautiful as spring
> When weeds, in wheels, shoot long and lovely and lush;
> Thrush's eggs look little low heavens …
> What is all this juice and all this joy?
> (Gerard Manley Hopkins, *Spring*)

This joy seems to be automatically conveyed to us through the sunlight, the waves of the sea, and the demure call of invisible birds. It springs up in our hearts as we awake to a new day as though to a new creation, like Adam in the poem of Mary Oliver, rubbing his eyes at the sight before him of the incredible gift of Eden. The joy and the playfulness of the Celtic artists who forged the *Book of Kells* can be seen on the pages of that masterpiece. It is a wonderland of mythical animals, exuberant patterns that become the hiding place for cats eating their tails, beasts with limbs like strands of chewing gum that pull out into long entwining strings, birds, ribbon-snakes and wrestling men. Joy is conveyed even by spare and rugged landscapes that threaten our senses. The question arises within us, 'How can it be that I love this scene, rugged though it be, and uncompromising?' It is a sort of challenged joy. The beauty of God is also there, stark and, at times, overpowering. A sight of distant mountains can stir in us a longing to be there in the experience of their grandeur and even of their challenge to the comfort of our senses. No wonder! We long, deep down within our souls, for the being of God, and something of that longing is communicated by the sight of great mountain scenery.

Creation can also present us with a sense of God's labour in the brokenness and sorrow we can experience. God laboured in creation and still does. In the third point of the *Contemplation for Love* Ignatius talks of the labour of God in creation, labour like a woman in childbirth. The negative things in nature, pain and suffering, disability, death and disfigurement, are often used as ways of destroying faith in God. But our pain is a reflection of his.

Most of all, for both the Celts and Ignatius, creation manifests mystery. Mystery is the hidden God within the things we perceive. It draws us by its very inaccessibility. It is often felt as a certain quality in a landscape or a room and, at times, in a church and its liturgy. Ruined places of worship often hold in their stones a sense of mystery and the closeness of the other world. Creation is God's lovescape. 'God saw all that he had made and found it very good.' All that he 'saw' was the product of his love. When he looked he saw the seascapes, the landscapes, the cloudscapes, his lovescape. A 'scape' is something you see, that you gaze at, that you wonder at, that your heart sails out over. That is how the Celts regarded creation, and Ignatius too was filled with the wonder of what he could see. He 'saw' God creating light, he gazed in wonder at the stars, he experienced the unity of creation as he stared into the water of the Cardoner river. The *Contemplatio ad Amorem* (*Contemplation for Love*) of the *Spiritual Exercises* comes from the heart of a man who could find God in the whole of creation in a way that bears comparison to the early Celtic saints. The wonder of God's presence and action was to be found in the commonplace, the everyday, the mystery of the obvious. It has been said that only the trivial mind needs the reassurance of supernatural events (in the sense of mind-blowing, amazing). It cannot see that everything, everything in the world around it is a miracle. Ignatius could see, and wanted everyone to see, the depth of God's presence in everything. Let us look in more detail at this prayer, the

34

Contemplation for Love which is placed in the last section of the *Spiritual Exercises*, the Fourth Week.

To describe this prayer in cold print suffers from the same disadvantage as trying to read the text of the *Spiritual Exercises* as a way of 'doing' the exercises. It is like staring at a skeleton as a way of seeing a living person (alas poor Yoric!). The *Exercises* are a 'doing' not a 'reading'. Maybe this is what makes them hard to take for many people – more like chewing a piece of biltong than a tender, juicy steak! Ignatius' statements are terse and pragmatic to the ear. In fact, though, this *Contemplation for Love*, as stated in the book, is the bare bones of a great love poem between ourselves, God and nature. But the poem is composed, the skeleton is enfleshed, from within the heart and soul of the person praying and contemplating. Ignatius was a man of action as well as contemplation. His notes at the beginning of the prayer talk of love as doing.

Once again we are confronted by that need to take responsibility, the need for commitment. Put your money where your mouth is! Give yourself, share yourself. In marriage, it is the giving of self to the spouse; in everybody, it is the gift of self to God.

But the giving is mutual, and God is the source of everything. What can we give to someone who is the source of everything? All we can give is ourselves, our love. The two notes at the beginning of this prayer show that we are in the realms of love. Creation is an expression of God's love and in the midst of creation we can find God and God's love present. But if the love is to be mutual then creation must respond to that love of God. In our spiritual life one of the hardest commodities to find is real encouragement. We don't seem to encourage each other enough in the things that are deepest to our life in God. So it is refreshing, at the beginning of this contemplation to find what is called a Composition of Place, that is, a setting, an *entrée* to the prayer, an entering into its spirit, body and soul. It seems, at first, to be a bit of a frolic: being aware of what we know to be the fact, that the whole court of heaven, angels, saints, and those loved ones who have gone before us, and, of course, the Trinity, are there for us. Lest anyone should feel that this is a formidable and forbidding (and judging!) array, we are left in no doubt that this multitude is rooting for us, wanting to help and encourage us.

To know that God and his whole entourage in heaven are standing on the terraces roaring in our support can do us no end of good. Our tendency can be to think of God eyeing us like a CCTV camera waiting for us to steal something off the shelves. But no, he is for us, and if God is for us who can be against? As already noted, such an awareness of the court of heaven is quite natural for the Celtic spirit. God is in no way an absentee landlord, making himself known only when he wants to collect rent money. He is more like a part of the family. In fact, there is a similarity in the attitude of the Celt and Ignatius towards the Lord of all things: an attitude of both reverence and familiarity. Where familiarity is truly based on love it is reverential.

Having given ourselves this fair wind in our sails, we move into the main body of the prayer which is trying to deepen our awareness of the relationship of God to creation. For although Ignatius was well aware of the awesomeness of a God who is above and beyond this world, he also finds God present in and throughout creation. The transcendent God is also immanent. It may seem difficult to put these two things together, but then we're dealing with God, who is way beyond our limited capacities of reason. There are four points or sections to this prayer.

The first section is a thanksgiving. Remember, he says, all the benefits of God, of creation, of salvation and how I myself have been gifted.

Remember. Memory constitutes us, plants and roots us. It places us firmly in the context of our whole life. Those events, places, people that were dear to us are not lost but stored in the temple of memory. To us, bound by time as we are, these things seem to have floated away and become lost. To God, all is present. Memories may be painful but by remembering we can bring them to the Lord, to the altar of healing. Memory is a prime factor in Ignatian spirituality. He strongly advocated a prayer of remembrance of the past day or week or whatever period we wish to recall. Memory reminds us what our experience has been. However, the facts of the past are useful only if reflected upon, in order, first of all, to be thankful for them, but more important, to learn from them. Dwell upon those bright moments of friendship or illumination when your step became lighter and your mind lit up. Give thanks to God for those moments, people, events. Learn too by the mistakes and failures which can show where we have dawdled off the path. Through all these successes and failures, if we but learn from them, God may be leading us.

The Celts were part of an oral society. Their histories, embroidered with imagination, were recited by the bards and poets and woven into the fabric of their lives. In the Christian era the monks took over their role, reciting the stories of the bible and salvation history. These things were written down in the manuscripts or engraved on the high crosses. Memory is of crucial importance to any Christian. But Ignatius is asking us to make it a personal history, too, of our own gifts, graces and salvation.

The second section (point two) of the prayer is to see how God dwells in creatures. The outlook of Ignatius coincides exactly with the Celts in this. The theologian Pelagius (later condemned for his refusal to accept Original Sin) could well have been describing the same point when he wrote:

> Animals roam the forests, birds flock in the sky, insects crawl in the grass, fish dash in stream and bay – and the Spirit of God informs them all. It is God's breath that gives life to every creature and to the trees and flowers and the grass of the field and the crops. That is why they are beautiful, because God breathes into them and looks at them. Nothing God looks at is ugly.

So said the Celtic writer and so too did Francis of Assisi, one of Ignatius' great heroes. Francis may well have been the source and inspiration for part of this prayer that we have been considering. Whatever its origin, it brings God into the very life of our senses, enabling us to see and feel his presence in blades of grass and the sound of the wind crossing a field of wheat; and in the stillness within nature. God comes to us in and through creation, not apart from it. The *Contemplation for Love* is Ignatius' Song of Songs for the earth and God's creation, his Song of the Earth. But it is not spelled out in his words, but is issued as an invitation to us to pray it. More than that, it will become our way of looking at nature and seeing God's Spirit everywhere at work in it. Our culture is estranged from the earth as a relationship of mutuality, and so does not come to understand the wisdom contained in the wonder and sanctity of a landscape, even a wild one. As the Jesuit poet, Hopkins put it:

The world is charged with the grandeur of God
It will flame out, like shining from shook foil:

But then he goes on, aware of our dislocation, from the earth:

Nor can foot feel, being shod.

What is to be gained from encouraging this sense of God present in the earth and all the elements? For the spiritual person it is, of course, an expression of a reality which cannot be seen, but is nevertheless real. The person standing in the sunshine on a glorious summer day, as described, for instance, in *Hebridean Altars*, feels the need to praise the sun-blessed day as a jewel dropped from God's hand. 'What a wonderful, beautiful mind this day must have come from,' he says, and asks that this loveliness pass into his spirit, and flow out from there as right-doing in his life, and the love which gives itself. God's Spirit is within us, and we can have reference to the Spirit to guide us.

So, one of the great attractions nowadays of Celtic spirituality is its attitude to creation. Our Celtic hermit, we read, wishes for a little hidden shack in a wild place for a house with birds around and a pool of water (to wash away sins!), standing next to a lovely wood, facing south for warmth and near a church and with sufficient clothes and food!

Well, who wouldn't wish for that! It could come straight out of a travel guide. Yet it does reveal the Celtic love of nature; and going along with that, an eye that notices the details of the surroundings. The hermit delights in watching Pangur, his cat, stalk a mouse as he himself stalks words to put on his page. It is the same eye for minute detail that is seen in the decorations of the pages of the *Book of Kells*, alive as it is with animal life. 'Pleasant is the glittering of the sun today upon these margins because it flickers so!' – scribbled by a scribe in an idle moment on the margin of a volume of Cassiodorus that he was copying. The Celtic saint was part of his landscape, not an intruder nor an owner, not an exploiter. His ambition was not to stand out from the surroundings, not to be a 'sore thumb' in the picture. In fact, he may not even have wished to be in the foreground at all, not the central figure. He wanted to fade into the scenery like a green knoll in a landscape of grass or a rock amongst crags. Only in this way could he absorb the real life of nature. The animal knows, with the accumulated wisdom of thousands of years of evolution, that if he be prey he must camouflage his presence. To exist in the fierce landscape of his choice he had to become part of it and present a smooth surface to the attacks of the biting wind or the gouging sea. Mary Low (*Celtic Christianity and Nature*) points out that many early poems, like Cetamon and *My Tidings for You*, don't actually make reference to religious things; but they show what she calls a primal sense of kinship with nature that gives them a sense of the power of God who is present, a primal sense on which we depend for our happiness and survival.

The close observation of nature with the wonder that ensues is itself a religious act. It is God's world, and this fact coloured all their way of seeing the earth and the whole of the cosmos. If God is the creator then creation, the work of his hands, must be essentially good. How could it be otherwise? When the Book of Genesis describes how God looked at the world of creation and 'saw that it was good', he was looking at the whole of creation, not just 'spiritual' bodiless realities. And this fact for the Celts was a matter of practical application, they found it in the things of nature around them. They were a largely rural people, living close to the earth, an earth imbued with the spirit of its maker just as a Beethoven symphony is redolent of the spirit of its composer. The search is on, these days, for the 'church without walls'. St Patrick discovered his faith when out of doors, working as a shepherd in the woods and mountains: 'I used to rise to pray, through snow, through frost, through rain' (Confession). And when explaining his faith to two princesses, daughters of a pagan king, he said (as we saw in chapter 1): 'Our God is a God of heaven and the heavens, of earth, sun and moon and stars. He dwells in the mountains and valleys, in earth and sea and everything in them, inspiring, quickening them all, over all, but supporting all.'

That would immediately appeal to the pagan hearers because they too believed that creation was good. They were brought up to regard the earth as sacred and to experience the holiness of the cosmos. Elsewhere in the Church all things pagan were regarded as evil and to be destroyed. Great energy was used in fulminating against the natural world, cutting down sacred trees, and despoiling sacred wells. Spirit was exalted over matter, heaven over earth and a wedge was driven between human nature and the rest of creation. The Celtic Church did not do this but accepted what went before it and blessed and baptised it rather than condemning and destroying it. St Samson of Cornwall, coming across a group of heathens dancing round their sacred stones and finding the dancers amenable to the Christian message, drew a cross on the stones and then joined in the dance.

In recent years there has been an enlightening reversal of some tendencies in evangelisation. We are so familiar with the heart-shrinking tales of the effect of missions on many native populations, abolishing their customs and substituting practices that were not essential to the message of the gospel but were western ways of thinking. So many babies emptied out with the bath water! In one of the General Congregations of the Jesuit Order in recent years a document expressed the conviction that God's Spirit is operative everywhere in the world, as well as in the Church as visible; and so, when a missionary goes to another land he or she does not presume to carry the truth to that people, but comes to find Christ and the Spirit at work there and help to make it explicit. Were we to stop there, seeing creation as all things bright and beautiful, we might be accused, as I have been, of ignoring the true picture of a suffering world.

The third section (Point three) of the *Contemplation for Love* gives a rather different slant on God's presence. God is now represented as one who is present in suffering and the labour of the earth, always at work for us in all created things. What is indicated here is not a static reality, but a dynamic one, and one which goes on now. When the mystic, Meister Eckhart, was asked, 'What does God do all day?' he replied, 'She lies on a bed giving birth!'

Quite a startling statement reminiscent of one description of this third point of the Contemplation: 'God loves me so much that he enters into the very struggle of life. Like a potter with clay, like a mother in childbirth … God labours to share his life and his love.' Creation is indeed a labour of love. This is a very dynamic image of God. God working, labouring.

And suffering. This comes to its fullness in the life and death of Christ, who showed us God present in our whole wrangling and striving existence; and who accepted the suffering that we are burdened with. My childhood idea of God creating the cosmos like a magician producing a rabbit out of a hat, is replaced here by a concept of creation as a labour, not like the labours of Hercules that, once completed, allow the labourer to relax, but something continuing, now, forever. 'What did I know, what did I know, of love's austere and lonely offices?' as the poet says. To someone who is praying in church Tagore says that God is not there, but out tilling the hard ground and with a person breaking up stones to make a path, his clothes covered in dust.

The last section (Point four) of the *Contemplation for Love* shows us God as Source of everything, an endless, inexhaustible Source.

The Fourth Point is to look how all the good things and gifts descend from above, as my poor power from the supreme and infinite power from above. God's love shines down on us like the rays of the sun on which we depend to give us light and warmth. How we rejoice when the sun comes out to give us warmth and light! The sun which is God never goes in! God showers gifts on us through creation. Like the water from a fountain, ever pouring out so that we can drink or take it for other uses, so is the love of God pouring down on us. He delights in us, in giving us gifts as a fond parent loves to give gifts to a child. God cannot do enough for us. The images are Trinitarian, the Sun representing God the Father of Light from whom all good things come down, the rays of the sun remind us of Ignatius' visions of the creation of light and Christ as the Sun. Water stands for the Holy Spirit.

If our praying of this great prayer has taken hold of our hearts we will feel the need to respond to God by giving ourselves to him in love and our service. We cheer when a Bride and Groom give themselves to each other at the altar for good and all. And love, in Ignatius' view, has to be two-way. But what can we possibly give back to a God?

41

You Father God have given, given, given
endlessly, earnestly, abundantly. You
embarrass me with kindness. I am but a speck
in your gaze, so how can I respond?
Take me, all of me, every last bit of me.
After all, you gave me me. Just
fill me with your Love and your Grace –
That's enough for me.

CHAPTER FOUR

Thorns in the Garden – The Tang of Sin

Ravaged, ravaged the earth,
despoiled, despoiled,
mourning and withering
(Isaiah 23:3–4)

Sin is always with us and won't leave us alone. It was there for the Celts as it was for Ignatius. Celtic Christianity had never a thought about Original Sin, perhaps until the squabble between Pelagius and Augustine. Their spirituality was more based on Eastern than Western ways of thinking. They saw creation as basically good (being the work of God's hands).

Yet there is a hair-raising tradition of penitential practice, asceticism, and protective prayer in their way of life. Despite the fact that they were not dualistic in outlook, there was a strong ascetical tone to their spirituality. They saw a good world, a good creation, as it were in bondage and being sabotaged to evil forces, like a country overrun and occupied by malevolent enemies. Christ came to free that country from the enemy. Our very nature seems to be fallen and corrupt. The Celts were good at holding paradoxes together and so they accepted the dark along with the light. Together with their sense of the basic goodness of creation and human nature they accepted sin, reparation, austerity and asceticism. They would have adhered to the expression in Romans 7 of the disastrous tension in the human being:

> I do not understand what I do; for I don't do what I would like to do, but instead I do what I hate. When I do what I don't want to do, this shows that I agree that the Law is right. So I am not really the one who does this thing; rather it is the sin that lives in me. I know that good does not live in me – that is, in my human nature. For even though the desire to do good is in me, I am not able to do it. I don't do the good I want to do; instead, I do the evil that I do not want to do. If I do what I don't want to do, this means that no longer am I the one who does it; instead, it is the sin that lives in me.

They were aware of the 'battle':

> The battle against many vices
> The battle against the body
> The battle against the devil.

Ignatius would have seen eye to eye with this. He battled against his vices, and strenuously against his body, and against the wiles of the devil. Sin was a reality for him from his own personal experience. At the time of his spiritual conversion at Manresa he was disgusted by his former sinful life of vanity, lust and aggression. He may have been involved in a killing. The method of dealing with his sexual sins was to suppress his lustful desires, helped by a vision he had of Our Lady holding the child Jesus. There was considerable psychological disturbance, which left him a victim of severe scruples especially with regard to his former sexual life. His method of coping with his scruples and other defects in his life was to use every exercise he could think of, praying for seven hours at a stretch and imposing severe penances on himself.

At first sight, Ignatius seems to be dualistic and anti-body. In his life it may be more assumed than referred to. His conversion leaves us with many questions about his attitudes to sin and salvation. At Manresa he went in for extreme penance, living in a cave, eating no meat, drinking no wine. He let his hair and nails grow, which was a form of punishment for the body he had been so proud of and so vain about. This is the principle of *agere contra* (literally, acting against). We can see here the same impulses as Pelagius would have admired, the strength of will to rule and win through to virtue. For him, and through him for his followers, the ultimate 'great deed' was doing away with self-will. But Ignatius gradually came to depend more on the grace of God than on his own power, realising that forgiveness is a gift of God, freely given and not 'earned' by our strenuous effort and penances.

In the *Spiritual Exercises*, the First Week is given over to the consideration of sin and evil. The Pilgrim (the person doing the exercises) is asked to be very aware of his or her own sins and evil tendencies, asking for a deep sense of shame and confusion, as though by such means we might overcome our sins and 'earn'

God's pardon. But that is not the object of the exercise. We can never 'earn' God's love or forgiveness – it is his free gift to us. Rather, it is a realisation that unless we are deeply aware of the sin in us, we will not be aware of our need of God's saving love and forgiveness. Unless you know you are lost you will not feel the need of the map!

The God of the First Week is a God of Mercy. We will not recognise our need of that mercy unless we can see our sins, looking at the foulness and the malice which any mortal sin has in it.

At the end of that First Week we are asked to meditate on 'hell', not in terms of flames and screams (which would be Ignatius' picture) but rather by imagining a world in which there is no God, no love, no Christ on the cross, no hand held out to help another, or held out in greeting. If you dig deep into that scene it can have a powerful effect. There are traces of it in the world around us, but to imagine a world in which there is only hatred and selfishness can make us determined never to go there. The description in the *Miracle on the River Kwai* (by Ernest Gordon) of the prisoner of war camp gives something of that picture, each man for himself, snatching what he could get regardless of the needs of the others. The caring love of one person turned that situation around, creating a Christian community in the camp.

The 'grace' of the First Week is conversion arising from the literally heart-breaking experience of being loved and forgiven. The essence of sin is the refusal to 'use' our freedom to give reverence and obedience to our Creator and Lord, refusal to allow God to be God in our lives. It is of the nature of sin that its effects are never confined to the individual but reach into the tissues of human society. The sins are described as 'foul' because they disfigure human life and conduct. Sin is not sin because it is forbidden – it is forbidden because it is foul, and affects relationships.

Ignatius uses images of sin, such as the soul imprisoned in the body of sin, in ways that we might not use nowadays – but the object is always to produce a realisation of our sinfulness. Although these images of sinfulness and inner evil have theological underpinnings they also reflect levels of sinfulness in Ignatius himself. He uses the imagery of his own time: the souls as in bodies of fire ... the wailings, howlings, cries, blasphemies against Christ etc. Was not this the dark imagery of his own mind? The use of willpower seems to be dominant, but his own experience taught him that it was the grace of God and the goodness of God that mattered.

Sin, in the *Spiritual Exercises,* is not confined by any means to the history of humanity on the earth. The pilgrim entering the first week of the retreat is asked first of all to consider what you might call a 'history of sin' which takes one right back beyond world history. There is, in the tradition, a 'sin of the angels' when Satan refused to obey God and was cast into hell along with other 'fallen angels', thereby constituting the whole empire of evil and temptation that the human race has to contend with in its life on earth. This counters the tendency to regard sexuality as the area most at risk in our lives and most conducive to sin. Angels have no bodies. Their sin was one of pride and refusal to commit themselves to the will of their Creator.

The sin of Adam and Eve is then considered as teaching truth, even if the story of the fall is mythological. And only at this point in the First Week is the person asked to consider, re-call, and react to his own sinfulness.

Always the devil is seen as the enemy who undermines the soul and human nature. Here the Celts and Ignatius come close together. In Celtic spirituality sin is the result of the penetration of exterior forces of evil into the human soul and will. Hence the predominance of 'protective prayers' to shield a person from the incursion of the evil spirit. So we get the tradition in the Celtic Church of penitential and ascetical practice which continues into our own day.

Many examples of this can be quoted. St Fintan 'never con-sumed during his time aught save the bread of woody barley and muddy water of clay'. St Kevin (of Glendalough) thrived on nettle soup and advocated it for all the inhabitants of Glendalough; but after a time they all began to be ill. You might be tempted to think that this was due to the diet of nettles, but no, it was dis-covered that the brother who prepared the soup was putting milk into it! So Kevin let up on the soup, but continued to be hard on himself. In his cell ('Kevin's Bed') he ate only nuts and herbs and drank water, had a stone for a pillow, wore skins and indulged in long prayers, reciting the office standing up to the waist in the water of the lough (cold!). And remained as healthy as a bee! Ita of Killeedy used to fast for three or four days at a time. Even being told off by an angel wasn't enough to make her change her ways; so the angel brought her (heavenly?) food. David of Wales plunged himself daily into cold water and remained in it long enough to subdue the ardour of the flesh (which, one imagines, must have been considerable!). It reminded me of a certain novice in our Jesuit novitiate who could be seen polishing his shoes with excessive vigour, as an antidote to bad thoughts! St David led an active life of prayer, teaching, genuflecting, caring for the poor, feeding orphans, widows, the sick … and so on.

The tradition of going to the desert was partly penitential. Jesus was 'driven' into the desert by the Spirit to be tempted by the devil. So the desert was a place to be tempted, or rather, tried, purged. In the desert, life was stripped of non-essentials (and sometimes even what we would think of as 'essentials'!) and it became a place where you meet with the Spirits, both good and bad. It was recognised as a place of penance and hardship, but mostly of confronting self and God and the 'spirits'.

Behind this is the realisation that our life on earth is not stable, and our human condition requires control and ordering. Just as an athlete must condition his or her muscles for running or jumping, so in the spiritual life the will has to be controlled and directed. Of course, this can lead to a very dualistic, anti-body, attitude of a Jansenistic type. For the Celts the dangers to the soul were the devil, the world and the flesh. The devil is obviously bad, the world is corrupted by sin, and the flesh … well, the less said about that the better! You were not supposed to live in harmony with the flesh, you subdued it. Hence 'mortification' which literally means 'killing' the bodily desires and passions (with the possibility of making us into spiritual vegetables in the process!). Is it possible that this sort of spirituality was partly responsible for the great hardships imposed on orphans, children in schools and institutions, by religious people?

The Celts were not dualistic but still recognised that there is a warfare with the devil. Demons everywhere in fact! The body does need to be curbed, or rather 'trained', just as an athlete needs to train.The Celtic High Crosses spell out their spirituality in stone. The powerful image of the 'O' of creation, the circle of the world, the crucified Lord with his hands held out embracing all people and bringing together redemption and creation.

As we saw, the Celtic mentality saw evil as something that beset you from outside of yourself, rather than being seated in your own psyche. The world, the air, is full of spirits of whatever sort, waiting to assault you and invade you. Hence the need for protection. Put on the armour of Christ. Many of the prayers are for the protection of God and the saints against the incursions of evil. The most famous of these is St Patrick's Breastplate (or *Lorica*, which means breastplate; and also called *The Deer's Cry*). This famous prayer calls upon God and the heavenly host for protection against the wiles of the Evil One. The heavenly host is that world which we cannot see but which is real. As the creed says, God is maker of all things visible and invisible. The people of the *Lorica* were familiar with this invisible world, it could shine through or otherwise impress itself on their perception. This other world was near and apprehensible to the Celts as to Ignatius.

The prayer, then, calls upon the cherubim and seraphim, the angels and archangels to come to protect the person praying. The great enemy is the demon, a wily foe who uses the circumstances of life and misfortune to cause havoc. This demon is real, both for Ignatius (who calls it 'the enemy of humankind') and for the Celtic Christian, and is powerful and a deceiver, called by St John 'the father of lies'. Ignatius warns that this enemy can appear in the form of an 'angel of light' (2 Cor 11:14); and so we need the help of the Light of Christ. For Christ too is invoked in this prayer in all the aspects of his incarnation, his life, death and resurrection and in his final coming in judgement. This is the subject of the Second Week of the *Spiritual Exercises* as we shall see.

It would not be right to consider the Celtic way of seeing sin as attack only from the outside, with no internal elements waging war against us. They were well aware of inner tensions and sinfulness. Part of the protection prayers contain expressions which ask the Lord to protect us against lust and anger and greed and other vices and tendencies that lean us towards false images and ways of thinking and knowledge that defiles us. There is an idolatry of the heart which we need to be aware of and pray to avoid.

Most of us nowadays have been brought up in an Augustinian world. Since the Fall we have inherited Original Sin so that all human beings are affected by it. We do have a sense of our sinfulness and 'Original Sin' is a way to explain why that should be so.

The essence of sin is the refusal to 'use' our freedom to give reverence and obedience to our Creator and Lord, refusal to allow God to be God in our lives. It is that which destroys the relationships that were established in creation and which Christ came to restore.

There seem to be two differing ways of thinking about the place of sin in our lives and both are present in the *Spiritual Exercises*. One is called a 'Test' mentality and the other is labelled 'Project'. The Test way of thinking is that what matters is the merit I accrue by keeping the law.

Man is created to praise, reverence and serve God our Lord, and by this means to save his soul. (Principle and Foundation)

There seems to be a flavour of the 'Test' attitude in the First Week, seeing sin as individual, judged by the keeping of the law. Merit is what matters, what is of value.

The 'Project' image, on the other hand, is one of co-operating in the project of God for creation. Sin here is social. Actually, sin always has social dimensions. You can keep the letter of the commandments without loving (Lk 18:18–27): the rich young man seemed to be a person who kept all the commandments yet did not seem to be gaining eternal life. In the teaching of Jesus, the one who makes use of and fulfils the law for his own peace and security of conscience will tend to turn the law into a criterion or instrument for judging those who, for one reason or another, have been unable to fulfil it (Lk 18:9–14: The Pharisee and the Publican). The 'Test' mentality is concerned exclusively with the salvation of one's own soul. This tends to obscure any concern with communal sin, concerns of justice and human rights. On the other hand, the project way of thinking allows these concerns to emerge and encourages them since its thrust is towards the building of the kingdom of God in this world (as it is in heaven) and reflects the constant preoccupation of Christ in his life to eradicate all elements of crime and injustice against the down-trodden, as also those areas of sickness that form a symbol of corruption and change which will ultimately be alien to the promises of the kingdom as fulfilled in heaven.

Both of these mentalities seem to have a place in the *Spiritual Exercises*, the first in the statement of the principle and foundation and the second in the Second Week dealing with the following of Christ in the work for the kingdom of God on earth.

A central meditation in the *Exercises* is called The Two Standards which wakens the awareness of the pilgrim to the presence of two opposed forces in the world, namely Satan and Christ. Each tries to win people to his 'standard', the devil by persuading them with desire for 'honours, riches and pride'; while Christ seeks to persuade with the opposite values of simplicity, poverty and humility. The devil and his minions know our human nature so well that often their workings are not detected. A modern example is the effect of advertising in our lives.

To help us to decipher which influence is which (Christ or devil) we can use the Rules for Discernment. These rules or helps make use of the terms Good Spirit and Bad Spirit. These terms cannot be totally equated with angel and devil. Rather they refer to any influence which moves us towards or away from God. But they do refer to the subtlety of the Evil One who knows how to attack at the weakest point, with a precise knowledge of human nature. Brian Swimme, in his book *The Heart of the Universe* points out that in the USA children will have been subjected to 30,000 adverts before they even start school, adverts created by experts in brain-washing. The chances are that our attempts to teach them religious principles after such brain-washing will have little effect on them. When one compares the pitiful efforts we employ for moral development with the colossal and frenzied energies we pour into advertising it is like comparing a high-school football game with World War II!

Sin destroys or distorts the relationship that we inherit from the Trinity. It can make us unwilling to pray, thus distancing us from the Source.

The figure stood in the darkness of the room.
I knew it well as one that I had made
With my own hands, of purest gold.
My heart was grieved to see it so wrapped round
And cobwebbed with the dust and grime of sin.
I took it gently down and blew upon its face
with the breath of my own mouth. The dust
rose up, an angry demon cloud
around the face of gold.
I wiped away the cobwebs and the grime,
and washed it to reveal its loveliness
shining like the sun that breaks the clouds.
I kissed it back to life and held it close.
'Sin shall not have you, you are mine,' I said
and in return it smiled to be redeemed.

CHAPTER FIVE

Christ of the Kingdom

It is not surprising that Christ should be central to any Christian spirituality and it is certainly true of both the early Celtic Christians and Ignatius. Christ emerges from the pages of the gospels as the true image or icon of the Father, and the Lord of all creation. All things were created through him and for him. Some would say that even if there had been no sin in the world Christ would have come. He is Lord of Creation, it is his rightful place. Christ is seen as the God-Man, the Son of God who came to show us the way to the Father. He brings the light of heaven into our dark and dour world, a good creation darkened by the satanic influences of sin.

The Celts knew a Christ who is both divine and human. He is the Second Person of the Trinity and his origin is from above. Born of the Virgin Mary, he was outstanding, memorable, a worker of miracles, a healer of the sick and a proclaimer of God's good news.

Early Celtic tribal life might be described as a hero culture, the great warriors performing deeds of valour. Great mythical heroes such as Cuchulainn were practically unconquerable, at times even unrestrainable. At the great feasts in the royal halls the warriors would boast of their achievements and the *filid* (poets) would tell endless 'rigmaroles' of the deeds of the great.

Not surprising, then, that Christ was seen as the hero *par excellence*. But his deeds were not those of warriors in the mythology. His great and surpassing deed was the Crucifixion. He was the one who saved his people. Just as the heroes of old saved their people by their prowess in war, so Christ saved his people by his life, death and resurrection. Cuchulainn fought off the enemies of Ulster who came to steal their treasured bull. Christ conquered sin and death for his people. The cross of Christ was evoked as a blessing and protection.

Ignatius was brought up in an atmosphere of courtly behaviour and war. He was proud of his *hidalgo* image. When recovering from the wounds he sustained at Pamplona, he dreamed of the feats of arms he would do to impress a lady. Fighting was in his blood. Heroes for him were war heroes. As he was drawn

more into the sphere of Christ's call to him his 'great deeds' became those in the service of Christ, deeds of penance and spiritual heroism. Christ became his hero and his loyalty transferred
to Christ as his leader. But the great deeds of Christ were not
those of war. His conquering was against the devil and against
the perpetrators of sin and evil. Ignatius began to call himself
'pilgrim'.

Christ was, for the Celts, a Liberator, freeing the creation from
the bondage of evil forces. He was an emancipator who draws us
into the glorious liberty of the children of God. He was *Christus
Victor*, triumphant on the cross, doing battle with the devil. We
can see this image on the High Crosses that still stand as evidence of the faith of that people. Christ had taken on the forces of
evil and defeated them, and it was his power over these evil
forces that were invoked in the protection prayers and the *caim*.

Nevertheless, the Celts did have the idea of sacrifice, not as
propitiation of an angry God, nor in forensic terms as ransom
for sin; but as the mystery of life coming out of death, and
progress out of suffering. God himself suffered on the cross, not
just Jesus. God came to humanity, and they come to God.

Christ was of absolute importance to Ignatius. The incarnation was the source and basis of his whole life and inspiration.

The whole middle section of the *Spiritual Exercises* (the
Second Week) is concerned with Christ, his call to follow him,
his life, teaching and miracles, the opposition he incurred, his
passion and death (Third Week) and then his resurrection
(Fourth Week). Christ is central to creation and salvation. Christ
is the one who is sent by the Father, coming from above and
going back to the Father. He is sent to do the Father's will. He
summons followers to help him to establish the kingdom. In re-
sponding to the call of Christ and helping in this project we are
ourselves sent. The accent is missionary. The Son is sent by the
Father, we are sent by the Son. In the process we are drawn into
the life of the Trinity. I, the creature, am sustained by Christ,
gifted for the mission. But there must be reciprocity. I wish to return what I have received, I want to mirror God's giving. Christ
is on pilgrimage for the salvation of the world. Christ is God in
the complexity of history, which is reflected in the phrase 'finding God in all things'.

The General Congregation of the Jesuits spoke about the call of Jesuits to the 'margins'. In geographical terms this may mean the missionary effort to distant places on the planet. But it can also mean two or three other things: people may be marginalised in various ways, by poverty, by disease, by lack of education and so on. 'Marginalised' can also mean separated from us by a different culture or religious belief (though which side of the equation is the 'marginalised' one is a matter of opinion!).

Celtic Christianity became missionary when the learning of the monasteries gave rise to the wanderings of monks in Europe, forming centres of spirituality and learning.

For both the Celts and Ignatius Christ was God and Man. Many of us were brought up (I'm talking about those born in the 1930s and 1940s) to see Christ as divine, the Son of God. The divinity was the dominant factor. The challenge for this generation was to discover the humanity of Christ. On the other hand, the apostles and disciples of Christ when he was on earth came upon him first of all in his humanity. They met him as a man, became friends with him and came to revere him and only gradually did they come to see that he was more than human whilst being truly human.

In the *Spiritual Exercises* Ignatius expresses both sides of the nature of Christ. He was the divine one who came down from above and would return there. His divinity is stressed throughout. When, at the age of twelve, he explained to his parents, Mary and Joseph, that 'I must be about my Father's business' as the reason why he had stayed in the Temple when they were searching for him, he seemed to be reaching beyond his human dimension and discovering his divinity. Throughout the gospels there are hints and rumbles of his divinity, voices proclaiming from heaven 'This is my beloved Son', statements that were indicative of his special relationship to God whom he called Father and Abba, and his proclamation in the dialogue with the Jews, 'before Abraham was, I am' which was sufficiently provocative for them to pick up stones to throw at him, accusing him of blasphemy. Other indications are plentiful in the gospels, his power over life and death (as in the raising of the widow of Nain's son and the restoring of life to Lazarus), and his power over the elements (as in the calming of the storm on the lake). But also there was the sense of something more than the limitations of humanity, the authority with which he spoke, the aura of transcendence.

All these elements were familiar to the Celts from their knowledge of the gospels, and particularly the gospel of John which they favoured for its contemplative colour. They would have entered into that Second Week of the *Exercises* with familiarity and excitement. The *Exercises* were above all an 'encounter' with Christ, and that is an experience that was familiar to them.

The stress on the use of imagination in praying the events of the gospel would feed into their imaginative souls. They would have no difficulty in 'seeing' Jesus and the apostles in their praying of the gospels. He would be there before them, would speak to them, and they to him, held by his eyes with their infinite depth. It took the disciples time to realise that the person of Christ was divine; the Celts were there already. But their Christ was a familiar figure, a person that they could encounter as a friend, one they referred to as 'Mary's Boy' (*Mac Muire*) with whom they spoke in an easy way without in any way losing respect or even awe. Christ was, for them, a companion and an intimate friend:

> Christ be with me,
> Christ within me,
> Christ behind me,
> Christ before me'.
> Christ is within me, the inner light. He walks with me:
> Christ walking with His apostles,
> And breaking silence he said:
> 'What is the name of this plant?'
> 'The name of this plant is the red-palmed,
> The right palm of God the Son
> And his left foot'(!)

In a similar way, Ignatius uses the term 'Colloquy' as a way to speak to God, the way a knight in his time might address his king. He wants us to talk in a familiar way, easily, without inhibition, but at the same time acknowledging within ourselves that we are addressing the King, or God or Christ. There is no loss of respect or loyalty. As we go to prayer Ignatius suggests that we stand for the space of an Our Father (i.e. a short time) before the place of prayer in order to become aware of what we are doing, and into whose presence we are entering, and to make this sense more forceful we might make some gesture, a bow or genuflection, to produce the right frame of mind for entering into an august presence. Nevertheless, the actual dialogue with Christ can be carried on in an easy and familiar way.

Ignatius was very conscious of the role of the body, and of creating the right atmosphere to facilitate our praying. If we are going to pray in a mood of repentance and awareness of our sins we don't sit outside on the veranda in the glorious sunshine, with a gin and tonic at our elbow, but rather we darken the room and kneel in a penitential position.

The Celts were very given to praying with arms outstretched, with frequent genuflections and signing of the cross. It is said of St Kevin in Glendalough that his oratory was so small that when he prayed his outstretched arms extended out of the windows on either side, and a blackbird made a nest in his hand and laid eggs so that Kevin had to remain in his prayer position until the chicks had hatched and flown the nest! But despite the often penitential attitude of the praying Celt, the Christ they spoke to was a familiar friend and brother whom they knew as Mary's boy. They felt the presence of Christ almost physically woven around their lives, being encircled by him, upheld, encompassed. This almost tangible experience of Jesus as a companion next to you, a guest in your house, a physical presence in your life, was perhaps the most striking way in which the Celts expressed their sense of God's presence, a presence in their ordinary life and work.

> Who are the group near the helm?
> Peter and Paul and John the Baptist;
> Christ is sitting at the helm
> directing the wind from the south.

This gives a picture of Jesus as not just very human but also close and accessible. This is a recurring feature of early Christian Celtic spirituality. A Welsh carol has Jesus as *The Big Little Giant who is Strong, Mighty and Weak*. A ninth-century hymn refers to

Little Jesus (*Jesukin*) nursed by me in my little hermitage. This stress on littleness and frailty of Jesus reflects their experience as a little people, frail, vulnerable and at the mercy of more powerful neighbours, not the triumphant and imperial Christ of the later Church. Jesus, then, is the humble Galilean fisherman who is a constant friend and companion as well as redeemer of the cosmos. This did not, however, mean an over familiar mateyness. Their prayers are not addressed direct to God in the vocative, but indirectly and invocationally. So, as noted above, the elements of awe and deference are maintained. God was the High King of Heaven, but kingship for them implied a gentle and beneficent Father, wise and just.

Ignatius' Christ is nothing if not approachable, a Christ that we find in the pages of the gospels as we pray them. There we encounter a Christ who draws crowds of people to him, healing their sick, talking to them in challenging parables and sayings. He speaks of things they know but hear anew, as he sits on a hillside or near the lake or by a well – places where people can meet him easily, and in the case of the woman with the haemorrhage, someone who seems to attract contact. He is a person who can draw people out, so that they will lay their problems at his feet. In fact, they feel that he knows their problems even before they mention them. He is compassionate, so much so that, seeing the tears of the widow of Nain, he is moved so deeply that he raises the widow's son. This prophet is certainly accessible, and when we pray to him, we can feel that attraction, that friendliness and love.

Christ was committed to his people. God so loved the world that he sent his only Son. He came to show them the Good News of his Father. He sat with them in their houses, visited them and talked with them. He ate with sinners, with us. He was involved in everything that involved them. One writer, looking at a Lowry painting of an industrial town, could see Christ in it:

> He looked and saw that it was Good.
> And the white skin of industrial leprosy
> became the white, white cloth of Resurrection.
> The throb of human life,
> even on the dunghill of industrial degradation
> became a living heartbeat.

And Christ walked the streets and shouted
over shuttles, drank beer in pubs and danced
at every corner. He roared with life, paraded
with a banner and lived full-bloodedly
among his neighbours, chanting the lays and folk-songs
of his people, mourning the deaths of mill slaves
killed in harness, slept in a bed of bone-invading
dampness, sheltered from seeping rain, corroding
weather, elbowed his way through jostling crowds
at market. He shared the evolution of mankind
and stepped up to his neck into the River
and never doubted this was what he came for.
He saw that it was good. Christ was engaged,
was risen in these people.

At its highest, Christianity is a demanding religion costing not less than everything. There is a large section of the *Spiritual Exercises* given over to the 'Call of Christ' during which the pilgrim considers how to adjust his or her life to express the love of Christ more fully, perhaps by changing their way of life or more simply, by deepening their faith and trust in God. This can lead to an 'election' or decision. Many Celtic Christians opted to live in a monastic setting or to find God in seclusion in rugged landscapes. The call of Christ demands total commitment, allowing nothing else but the love of God to be its life and treasure. The love of God is, as it were, switched so as to fill the whole screen of the computer. The idolatry of the material world, and all its addictive attraction, is pushed away.

Jesus calls men and women to come under his standard, to stand by him through thick and thin, and if necessary to give life itself rather than deny him. Jesus calls us. But he leaves us in no doubt as to the consequences of our choice. Following him must overrule love of family or a comfortable or 'successful' life. It will also involve 'death' to our ego-dominated ambition. It is our own *kenosis*. It is serious business. We are 'called off the bench' as they say in football, committed fully to the battle of life. The Christianity of the gospels is one of commitment. Both the Celts and Ignatius would recognise the imperative nature of that call and would want, in their lives, to respond to it. But the absolute nature of the call demands that the pilgrim should follow Jesus even in his passion. The Third Week of the *Exercises* involves the pilgrim in the passion of Our Lord.

The Samurai, a Japanese convert to Christianity in the novel by Endo, is sent to Rome to deepen his grasp of his new religion. On the way he passes through countries which are Christian, and everywhere he saw, on walls, in churches, standing by the wayside, representations of Christ crucified. It proved to be a real stumbling block to the Japanese sensibility. Weak humanity, to him, was a despicable thing, and Christ on the cross represented total weakness. But the crucifix is the most commonly represented symbol in Christianity and at first this appalled the Samurai.

Praying the passion of Christ is the work of the Third Week of the *Spiritual Exercises*. Answering the call of Christ to follow him and work for the kingdom of God, the pilgrim then has to show his or her total commitment by following him in the passion, so that having walked with him in the work of the kingdom he or she should walk willingly the way of the cross.

Jesus insisted that if you wish to follow him you had to take up your cross (and Luke says 'daily') as part of your following. The cross then, may not mean great physical suffering, although for some people that is required of them. But normally it means following the Lord in our commitment to the daily grind and to such suffering as our relationships may impose on us. We can join our pains to the passion of Christ and they then become redemptive.

St Ignatius, on the way to Rome with his companions, spent time in a little chapel at La Storta. He prayed to the Father saying: 'Place me with your Son, place me with your Son.' The vision of the Son that he saw was Christ carrying his cross. The Father acceded to his request. For some, as St Paul claimed, the cross was a stumbling block to faith, but for many, paradoxically, it was a drawing point.

Hither then, last or first
To hero of Calvary, Christ's feet –
Never ask if meaning it, wanting it, warned of it – men go.
(Gerard Manley Hopkins, *The Wreck of the Deutschland*)

The passion was seen by the Celts as the heroic act by which the hero, Christ, saved the world from sin. In the retelling of it the poet Blathmac expressed with typically vivid imagination, the physical details:

How I lament the crucifixion of Christ!
Alas for anyone who has seen the Son of the living God
stretched fast on the cross!
Alas, the body possessing wisest dignity
now plunged into blood!
Hands were laid upon the face of the King
who was severely beaten.
O hideous deed! – the face of the Creator spat upon.
His cross was placed between the crosses
of the condemned
And he was raised upon the cross in pain.
King of the seven holy heavens,
when his heart was pierced,
wine was spilled upon the pathways,
the blood of Christ flowing through his gleaming sides.
They presented him with a parting drink.
Hurrying him to his death,
they mix (dastardly deed!) gall for him with vinegar.
He raises a beautiful protesting voice
beseeching his holy Father:
'Why have you abandoned me, living God,
to servitude and distress?!'

The invitation in the *Exercises* to walk with Jesus as he carries his cross to Calvary is one which would appeal to the Celtic mind. As the poem above shows, he would feel the plight of Christ deeply and himself suffer, not for the sake of suffering itself but for the love of Christ. Just as Christ showed his love for us by his death on the Cross, his complete emptying or *kenosis*, so we can show our love for, and commitment to, the Jesus of the passion by our own attachment to him as he dies for us. This is not a tragedy but the inevitable fruit of our following of Christ and if we refuse to enter into the passion we refuse to follow the call of Christ. One of the great challenges in the *Exercises* is the section called Three Kinds of Humility, the third of which states:

'I so much want Christ's life to be my own that I opt for poverty with Christ poor, insults in order to be closer to Christ insulted, and to be considered worthless or a fool for Christ, rather than be thought wise. I want his experiences to be reflected in my life.' The passion of Our Lord was such a reality for the Celtic people and Jesus was so close to them that they really felt they had to suffer with him and suffer willingly.

The passion is an essential part of the Christian life. In terms of the *Exercises,* following Christ in his suffering was seen as a confirmation of the decision, the 'election', of a way of life that expressed the pilgrim's love of Christ and willingness to follow him. The word 'confirmation' means literally a strengthening that would enable the pilgrim to fulfil the great desire expressed in their election.

Following Christ in his life and death leads to following in the joy of the Resurrection and a deep awareness for both Ignatius and the Celts of living in the presence of the Risen Lord.

> To read the words 'Come follow Me'
> just written in a book (although a sacred book)
> can be a shock; to hear them echoing
> in my own heart-space, to realise they call to *me*
> is quite another thing, with far more serious tone
> causing my heart to stop, a tingling in the bone.
> I pretend it is not there, I just imagined it,
> romantic call to arms, beckoned from the bench
> into the Arena where lions roar and chew.
> But ... but ... but ...
> But lead on, I will follow.

CHAPTER SIX

Imaginative Praying

Prayer is the attention, each to the other, of friends and lovers. It conveys the expression of the life of the creature, the appeals, the desires, the failures, the sobbing cries; and the listening of the Lover who is God, his ear ever attentively waiting to hear the long motet of human life. Christ prayed to his Father to tell him of the life of human striving that he had undertaken, and seeking the grasp of the parental hand to guide him.

At times, the praying person seems to be praying into empty space (how often have we not felt this?); but the Lover God is never asleep when his child is crying. A mother loves to hear the babble of her child, however garbled and childish, telling her something of the life of that growing soul.

One of the strongest roots in the tree of Christianity – of all religions in fact – is prayer. It is the necessary communication between the life of heaven and of earth. It may not be confined to words. When a baby smiles into the face of the mother there is a deep communication of love. When Christians pray they adopt a definite pose, kneeling, standing, sitting or lying flat; and certain gestures will assist them to express what they are saying in words or thinking.

The Celtic Christians prayed with their bodies, holding arms out in the shape of a cross, genuflecting, bowing, walking around to outline a circle of protection. They sought always the best place and position, where the veil between the soul and God was thinnest.

The Celtic day was full of God. Every activity was assigned its God-place and its blessing. Everything they did, marked with a prayer or blessing, reminded them of the presence of their Lord and Maker and of the angels and saints. So their actions themselves gave glory and blessing to their Maker. There was a prayer for rising and going to bed, for washing, dressing, milking the cow and asking for protection from the incursions of the evil one. Thus the person prays that as he or she lies down at night he or she will be accompanied by Mary and her Son and the bright angel Michael. Starting the fire in the morning had its prayer, again accompanied with the angels and shielded by the Holy Son of God from fear of the enemy or terror from anyone under the Sun.

Fishing was a serious occupation for many people living on the coasts of Ireland or Scotland and there was a little ritual of blessing to be said antiphonally by the whole crew, using a form of repetition which is to be found frequently in the prayers of the Celtic people and the structure of the Trinity:

Helmsman:	Blessed be our boat.
Crew:	God the Father bless her.
Helmsman:	Blessed be our boat.
Crew:	God the Son bless her.
Helmsman:	Blessed be our boat.
Crew:	God the Spirit bless her.
All:	God the Father, God the Son, God the Spirit Bless the boat.

In a similar way the hatching blessing is immersed in a ritual, said and performed by the woman (and it has to be a woman) as she goes 'sunwise' with her basket of eggs to place them beneath the 'clocking' hen, 'clocking' being the sign of motherhood. Jesus had likened himself to a hen who would gather the people under his wing as the hen gathers her chicks. 'Sunwise' is a way of enlisting the energy of the all-nurturing sun behind her as she goes to the nest. The woman puts her hand to her breast, thus involving her own motherhood (actual or potential) with that of the hen. In this way she makes a connection between her own body and the generative power of the Creator, and the woman's nurturing power enters into the work of the hatching chicks. The woman's role is thus priestly, linking the divine to the human world.

This lovely ritual shows the Celtic way of seeing God at work in the whole of his creation. It is holistic and brings together sacred and secular.

The prayers often convey a use of imagination in the way they are expressed. Christ is seen walking with his disciples and asks them the name of a plant and then explains that it is called the 'red-palmed', the right palm of God the Son and his left foot!

Poetic insight and creativity are qualities of the Celtic spirit. John O'Donohue maintains that the human capacity for imaginative creativity stems from our likeness to God, a sharing in the divine creativity and imagination that gave rise to creation and continues to do so. God's desire for us is that we play out, in writing, painting, sculpting and any other creative ways, his image in us.

Imagination, that powerful faculty, gives a sacred colour to both Celtic and Ignatian prayer. It allows for a great freedom that enables a person to see 'what might be' beyond what is and always has been. It brings together in a balance the heart and the mind, feeling and thought. It allows us to walk in the precincts of the divine, opening to us the treasure-trove of the Trinity. The image of God in us is like a great paint-box waiting to be used to create a wonderful tableaux of colour. Imagination opens up for us new possibilities, new hope and a Jacob's ladder towards God and heaven.

Imagination in prayer has a wonderful capacity for clothing cold thought in warm flesh. When used in the context of the gospel truths it can open new revelations to us. Working through suggestion, it respects and presents the mystery but in a way that is tangible and confrontational. In imaginative prayer you meet the Christ of the gospel face to face, confirming the mystery of the incarnation and seeing through the materiality to the divine. 'Follow Me.' The imagined call is known to be from the depths of the creative soul through which God works in us. We are touched by that strange divine attraction that gives the imagined call such authority and power, drawing us with an irresistible magnetism. Possibilities open up, new questions arise. The horizon expands at the edges of our vision. Useless for us to ask, with Mary, 'How can this be?' The angel simply points to the wild extravagance of God. 'Nothing is impossible with God.' And you are drawn into that impossible wildness.

A Celt praying would use his imagination to see the cross, for instance, and ask the Lord to help him know the passion more deeply; and hear Christ reply, 'Live in the spirit of my dying.' Or he would imagine the Lord knocking at his door and telling him to come in.

Imagination played a great part in the conversion of St Ignatius from the rather dissolute life he was living before he was wounded to becoming a disciple of Christ. He had a strong imagination and while he lay immobile on his bed of recovery it was inevitable that his imagination was given free play. He imagined himself jousting for the favours of a lady, and winning battles against the Saracens. This imaginary world would have been furnished with themes taken from the reading of the romances written by Amadis de Gaul and others, but in his brother's house where he was convalescing (and where we can detect the pious influence of his sister-in-law, Magdalena) there were no novels and he was given the *Life of Christ* by Ludolph of Saxony and the lives of the saints to read. As he gained a taste for this spiritual reading his imagination followed suit. The lady he now jousted for was Mary the mother of Jesus. He saw himself performing great deeds of asceticism trying to emulate the saints and their deeds.

It is not surprising, then, that praying the gospels which became a large part of the praying in the *Exercises*, took an imaginative form. The pilgrim is asked to imagine the scene and use his or her senses in the imagination. The person praying would see the scene, see the people present, see the actions done, hear the words said and any other relevant noises (the noise of a crowd walking the road, for instance), hear the words spoken from heaven, touch the hem of Christ's garment or feel his touch as he washes the pilgrim's (your!) feet, taste the bread and wine, smell the straw in the stable of the nativity or the smell of the perfume with which he was anointed at Bethany and so on. Imagination gives form to thought, putting you in touch with situations in a concrete way that thought by itself could not attain. Of course, imagination needs to be checked, and like any prayer it needs to be put to the scrutiny of the Spirit.

To gain an impression of the use of imaginative prayer in the *Spiritual Exercises* we can imagine a pilgrim – let's call him Mark – reporting to his director in the 30-day retreat. He had been praying using the text of Mark 10:46–52, the cure of the blind beggar, Bartimaeus. In his imagination he was the beggar and spoke his words:

I found myself by the wayside, outside Jericho, sitting begging, wrapped in my cloak. I kept wanting to see the surroundings as, you know, we're meant to do in a contemplation, but I couldn't because I was blind. My cloak was important, because it could be cold at night, and anyway, I need the cloak to pad my thin bottom from the hard stone at the side of the road. People passing by kick me as I sit there and swear at me, so the cloak is a bit of a protection. And I often conceal money inside it, so people don't get the impression I have enough money and so don't give me anything. The blindness kept me from making contact with the outside world – not entirely of course, I had my other senses – but as a main channel for seeing what's outside me, and come to that, channelling information from outside to the inside. I know blind people overcome their blindness by having a guide dog and do a lot by touch and sound; but for me, not having my sight is like being enclosed in a box. But also, I feel I'm leading a life that is blind. My spirit is blind. And it's a lonely life.

When I heard the crowd going by, and knowing – how did I know? – that it was Jesus, I began to shout, just shout to get attention, but then yelling, 'Jesus, help me, help me!' I felt a bit hopeless and helpless. Why should he help me?

Then he stopped. Stopped! You could hear the shuffling noise stopping, and a sort of quiet as people wondered why he had stopped. I could hear my heart beating. I heard him say, 'Bring him over here,' and boy, did I leap up! I threw the cloak aside, it was keeping me back. I thought about that cloak afterwards. It seemed to represent my life up until then, something wrapping me around with comfort and protection, but getting in the way when I wanted to move towards Jesus. So I threw it aside, and ran to him. That may sound odd, since I was blind, but anyway I ran. And I knew when I had reached him ... I could feel his presence.

He asked, 'Mark, what can I do for you?'

What can I do for you! Can you imagine that? *He* asked *me*, 'what can I do for you?' What a reversal of all my religious upbringing! God and Jesus had always been *demanders* until that moment: 'Mark, you must do this, Mark, you must do that, you mustn't do that, you mustn't do this, find out what Mark is doing and tell him to stop. If you enjoy it, it's wrong!' Now here was this God-figure, Jesus, saying to me, 'Mark, what do you want me to do for you?'

Excuse me ... I'm a bit choked up ... I said, 'My sight! My sight!'

And he simply said, 'Go, your faith has saved you.' My faith! My faith had been like a sort of jellyfish, you're not sure it's there until it stings you. It all seemed so *easy*.

'Easy?' prompted his director.

'Yes, casual: You want your eyesight, well, here's your eyesight!'

'What was it like, Mark, getting your sight back?' asked the director.

'Well, like having a light switched on – suddenly you can see everything, colours, shapes and things, like a light inside ... a bit frightening really. Like the light being switched back on after a power cut. You look around the room and suddenly realise that the furniture is all rubbish and needs changing. I was seeing myself in a new light. Things need changing.'

This powerful faculty, imagination, can give form to our concepts making them visible, tangible, audible, totally accommodated to our senses. God can communicate to us through it. Joan of Arc, faced by the judges at her trial, said she heard the voices from heaven telling her what to do. The judge sneered that it was her imagination. 'Of course,' she said, 'that is how God communicates to us.' Imaginative prayer was found by Ignatius to be a powerful tool for 'enfleshing the mystery' and so, in the *Spiritual Exercises*, it is recommended as a form of prayer when praying the events of the gospel.

It is a freeing faculty, allowing us to 'see' the invisible, and touch the intangible and know the inapprehensible as Francis Thompson describes in his poem 'O World Invisible'. It can also allow us to make the jump from the imagined event in the gospel into our own present world and see, as Thompson has it, Christ walking on the water of Thames rather than Gennesaret!

Prayer, of course, can be described in many ways and has many forms and functions. I think it has a particular form in the *Spiritual Exercises*. First of all, it is an awareness of the presence of God and contact with him. That awareness calls for a deepening of the relationship with God and a corresponding deepening of love; and finally, it moves the praying person towards a commitment to Christ by dwelling upon the mysteries of his life through contemplation of the gospels.

So, though I have stressed the importance of imaginative prayer in the *Spiritual Exercises,* it is not the only form of prayer that is recommended there. Ignatius would recommend any prayer form that makes the presence of God palpable for the person at prayer. Meditation is a prayer in which material is thought out or mentally processed and it has its place in the *Exercises*.

The sense of God's presence is a basic requisite of prayer in the *Exercises*. The pilgrim entering into prayer is recommended to 'stand before the place of prayer for the space of an Our Father' (meaning, a short time). Thus he or she creates a 'sacred space' into which she then enters with full reverence. This is a simple awareness exercise of the presence of God in that sacred space. It helps too if the pilgrim makes a simple gesture, a bow or a sign of the cross, or raising of the hands, in order to heighten that sense of presence. A person entering a Catholic church will often genuflect to acknowledge the presence of Christ in the sacrament in the tabernacle. It is, again, an awareness exercise, a reminder of the sacredness of the place and of the activity of prayer that she is about to engage in. This awareness of the presence of God provides a firm foundation for the effectiveness of the prayer. If we do attain a deep awareness of the presence of God, and stand before him, the impact can be powerful. This awareness is the factor which shifts the prayer from a head knowledge into an encounter with God and knowledge of the heart where motivation for action and change is rooted.

This becomes especially true in the contemplations of the life of Christ in the gospels. This is where the imagination and the use of imaginative prayer comes into its own. The imaginative meeting with Christ in the gospel narratives can involve the pilgrim in a deep and heartfelt love of Christ and desire to be with him and follow him. This, in turn, can lead to a strengthening of the desire to act in our lives for the kingdom of God in ways which become clear to us as we see Christ's desire for the world and its people. The precise way in which we are called to act for the kingdom will arise as we pray using texts about the call of the apostles in the gospel, such as the call of the first four disciples in Luke 5, or the call of Matthew in Matthew 9.

Prayer, ultimately, is about encounter with the person of Christ and with the presence of God. Many of the recommendations in the *Spiritual Exercises* are aimed at promoting that contact and sense of presence. Standing before the place of prayer for a short time is a moment of awareness of the presence of God, seeing how God is looking at me is seen as drawing me into the sphere of God's vision. Just as the baby smiles at her mother, so we too can smile at God. It switches a light on in our souls and transfigures us.

One or two recommendations for praying:

- Try the smile when entering into prayer. Or bow, or make a gesture with your hands to help you to be aware of the presence of God.
- Take any event in the gospel and place yourself in it in your imagination, set the scene, see the persons, see what they do, feel features of the scene, the crowd or the river, hear what is said and so on.
- Make a 'colloquy', talking to God.
- End with an 'Our Father', and then reflect back on the prayer.

> *The Smile*
> When a baby smiles
> a mother's heart turns over.
> A smile is a prayer,
> locking hearts together,
> a prayer without words
> but worlds of meaning and love.
> Why then do we not smile at God?
> She cannot fail to answer.

CHAPTER SEVEN

Mission and Learning

As a boy I attended a Jesuit school. The classes there were not called First Year, Second Year, Third Year etc. They gloried in such names as Figures, Rudiments, Grammar, Poetry and Rhetoric. It was a reflection of the strong influence on St Ignatius of his university training in Paris at the time when humanism was becoming the order of the day there, as it was in many other centres of learning. It seemed to suit Ignatius' temperament. When he realised that the college he first attended, Montaigu, was ruled in a more old-fashioned way, he moved after a year to another college, Sainte-Barbe, where the regime was more to his liking. As a result, some characteristics of humanism put a definite stamp on the spirituality of the Jesuits and how they saw education. Although humanism did not exist as a recognised style of life until well after the coming of Christianity to the Celtic countries, it agrees well with their way of living and believing.

Celtic monasticism was open to visitors and had an evangelistic bent. The monasteries had become centres for the pursuit of learning, so that a people who had been more or less illiterate became copyists and writers in the monastic *scriptoria*. Since there was no division between sacred and secular these centres preserved much of the ancient learning, both Roman and Greek. Students were attracted from all over Ireland, from Britain and the continent. The art of the ancients was kept alive.

Throughout the so-called Dark Ages the celtic monasteries were practically the only repositories of scholarship and learning. In the centuries of the barbarian invasions they promoted the acceptance of God's law and a morality that helped to control the lives of thousands of people in Europe. But there was another thing that they introduced – an emphasis on the cultivation of the mind. The newly-established monasteries on the continent helped to preserve the learning (and the documents) of classical antiquity and also the early Christian writings. They had libraries containing many ancient manuscripts which would have disappeared had it not been for the assiduous efforts of the monks to preserve them and pass on the learning they contained. This love of learning and culture is evident in the schools established by the Jesuits. At first, in the very early years, the Order was largely missionary, and adapted to the needs of many different places and peoples. This corresponded to the expressed nature of the Jesuits, as missionaries ready to go to any part of the known and unknown globe to bring the love of God to the people. The film, *The Mission*, shows clearly the love of culture and artistic expression of those missionary Jesuits. As the Celtic Christians did on the continent of Europe, so the missionary Jesuits did in various parts of the world. It is said that by the 8th century every European kingdom employed Irish scholars as advisors to the royal court.

It is no surprise to find that this love of learning and the regard for the individual have their influence on the *Spiritual Exercises*. The *Exercises* are not simply an academic thesis but are tapered to the whole person, body and soul. This holistic way of proceeding takes its stand at the level of experience. The style is affective, moving the heart and emotions and leading to action or the resolve to act. But the heart is not allowed to run off on its own without reference to the head; they work together in tandem. There is not much use in knowing what Jesus did and said if it makes no difference to you in your life. St Ignatius and the early Jesuits used the *Exercises* to 'help souls', which meant helping the person. They did not try to 'teach' people and instil spiritual values without regard for their general wellbeing. They helped in the hospitals amidst the squalor and dirt of such places in those days, trying to ameliorate the condition of people suffering from syphilis and plague, in danger themselves of contagion. In later times the poet Gerard Manley Hopkins died when he caught the plague while helping those suffering from it in Dublin where he is buried. The group around Ignatius also begged in order to get money for food for the poor and hungry of the neighbourhood.

In the life of St Brigid and other Celtic saints you find exactly the same spirit at work: a desire to help the whole person, body and soul. Her institution in Kildare fed over a thousand people each day as did other monasteries. The precept of hospitality was strongly advocated and observed.

A clean guest-house with a warm fire,
A good bathroom and a sofa to dream of …

Bringing the knowledge of Christ to the people of the world ('Go and teach all nations …') meant going beyond the confines of recognised civilisation and moving into unknown, unexplored territory. Christ himself often broke the bounds of what his Jewish faith demanded. His public life was that of an itinerant preacher, moving from place to place. One morning before dawn he went out to seek a lonely place where he could pray, probably up a local hillside. He needed to find his space. But his space was soon invaded. Peter and others came searching for him, obviously not realising that Jesus himself, Son of God though he was, needed to pray to retain that contact with his Father who was the very inspiration and motivation of his life and action. Peter was probably like many of us who find it difficult to see why Christ should need to pray at all, since he is normally seen as the recipient of prayer, not the one praying! On finding him, Peter exclaimed, 'They're all waiting for you down there.' 'OK', said Jesus, 'but let's go somewhere else, to another town.' He needed, apparently, to spread his wings and scatter the seeds of the Word far and wide. He seemed to want to start fires here and there, rather than staying with one fire to put more fuel on it. He had come to set fire to the whole world.

Like a schoolboy playing truant, Jesus moved out of the Jewish territory into gentile lands, across the lake to the Gadarene country. He argued with a Syro-phoenician woman, thereby breaking two strict rules, talking to a Gentile (especially in public) and a woman (especially in public)! He led his followers to Caesarea Philippi and through Samaria, bending the boundaries and the rules.

Was this why both the Celtic Christians and the followers of Ignatius became great travellers in the attempt to spread the word about Jesus?

At a time when the world was being explored and horizons were being expanded the followers of Ignatius were seeking to expand their horizons to spread the good news of the kingdom of God. A phrase used of Ignatius and his first companions was 'one foot in the air', meaning 'always on the move'. It is even written into the Constitutions of the religious order he founded and called 'Companions of Jesus' (later nicknamed 'Jesuits') that the vocation of the Jesuit was to travel to different places (*diversa loca peregrare*), going wherever they were sent and wherever there was need. Over the years, the excursions to the missions grew. They travelled all over Europe and to the limits of the then known world to spread the good news of Christ. Missionaries of all sorts have travelled as the Jesuits did. I quote the following examples because they are familiar to me from my own Jesuit background.

It would take an underground bunker of the sort we see in films of the Battle of Britain, to keep track of the movements of these first Jesuits. Men like Pierre Favre who, at the age of forty, died of exhaustion in Valladolid in Spain, had travelled from Worms to Speyer to Mainz, on to Portugal and back to Cologne in Germany and back again to Portugal. All on foot! He was making for Rome when he died. Others of his contemporaries made journeys all over Europe at a time when there were no high-speed trains nor cars, and certainly no easyJet flights. Of course, there were exceptions to this incessant movement. Rodriguez, chosen for the Indian mission, contrived to stay in Lisbon!

Of the original ten men with Ignatius four went East, the best known being Francis Xavier, whose mileage was incalculable. The film, *The Mission*, reminded us of the work done in South America by the Jesuits. As often as not they had to explore the territories they were evangelising. There was no limit to their journeying nor to the ingenuity in the work they were doing, adapting their way of life to that of the people they were helping. Matteo Ricci (1583) dressed as a Buddhist monk, known as Li-Ma-Ton in China, to facilitate contact with the people there. De Nobili became a sannyasi guru in India for the same purpose. It was a lesson in inculturation that the Church has only just relearned!

Jesuits made astonishing journeys from India to China, discovering, in the process, Tibet. In 1602, Bento de Goes, a Jesuit brother, crossed the Hindu Kush and part of the Gobi desert and reached Sucheu in China after three years travelling, trying to find a land route to avoid the Portuguese-dominated sea route from one country to the other. After de Goes, Antonio Andrade viewed the plains of Tibet from the summit of the Mana Pass, 18,000 feet up, discovering that country for the West.

These few examples can serve to show the surging spirit of quest that filled those companions of Inigo of Loyola, and still fills them today. It was a spirit that was willing to give unsparingly of energy, interest and even of life itself when that was required of them. There have been numerous martyrs among them, not only in the dim and distant past but even in our own times.

Their exploration was not confined to physical travelling; the mind was also a land to be explored and research was part of their educational effort. Jesuit schools have existed around the globe. At one stage in my own training I had to attend a science course in a 'tech' in Oxford. I was dressed as a cleric, and in the class were students from different countries. One of them passed me a piece of filter paper with words scratched on it, something like 'tan tomb err go sac ramen tum,' which I eventually deciphered as *Tantum ergo Sacramentum*, Latin words we used to sing at the ceremony of Benediction. Although he was a Muslim he had been educated by Jesuits in Egypt!

This energetic, humanistic desire to travel into unknown territory has had very far-reaching results. There are Jesuit names on the moon, put there by astronomers of the Order. It is not surprising that a best-selling novel, *Sparrows* by Mary Dora Russell was based on an imagined journey by Jesuits to a planet called 'Rakhat'!

People have always been willing to die or suffer in prison, for great causes, in wars, to promote justice, for political ends. What was the cause for those Jesuits?

The answer is simple: part of their training was to do the *Spiritual Exercises* which Ignatius had written down as a help to people wanting to advance in the service of God. It was in response to what they had found in the *Exercises* that they were committed to doing whatever was required of them for the spreading of the kingdom of God. Ignatius was so sure of the power of the *Exercises* to form his followers that he presumed their ardour and faithfulness. When asked to stipulate a more thorough and precise prayer regime for the professed members of the Order, he said they were formed in the *Spiritual Exercises* and so did not need anything further. If that was their grounding it was a treasure for life. The holistic approach of the *Exercises* resulted in a commitment of the person, body and soul, to Christ and the work of Christ.

A look at the First Week of the *Exercises* can give us a sense of the importance of the holistic approach. This First Week is concerned with sin, its nature, and destructiveness. Maybe this is why, for some, the *Exercises* have a dire reputation. The image of the black-robed Jesuit in James Joyce's *Portrait of the Artist* leading a school retreat and scaring the hell (literally!) out of the pupils had a scarifying effect.

While the intellect can wrestle with what might be termed 'the history of sin', namely the sin of the angels, the sin of Adam and Eve, and the effect of serious sin on a person's life, the main thrust of the week is to recognise one's own sin and experience the shame and sorrow evoked from that awareness, leading from there to a deep and happy awareness of God's forgiveness and love.

This is more than a mere passive remembrance of what one's sins have been, a sort of shopping list of mainly historical interest. It is a present experience of what destruction these sins caused and are causing in my life. Being distasteful, such experience demands 'hard chewing' and constant repetition. I look at Christ on the cross ('I helped to put you there'), I ask, again and again, for a deep sense of my sinfulness, and I make the atmosphere conform to the mood I am trying to enter. I don't, therefore, skip around in the sun in the garden, in fact, I close the shutters in my place of prayer to expel the light; I don't sit and watch comedy on the TV, or read novels. I keep my thoughts set upon the objective, reminding myself of the elements of my prayer before going to bed and when I wake up. I may cut down on food and drink to show my sincerity in the effort to know my sinfulness. I pray in dark parts of the chapel and pull the curtains in my room as I pray. I kneel or sit or lie on the floor, whichever position helps towards my deepening prayer.

All this is in recognition of the holistic approach. The heart cannot feel shame and sorrow for sin if the body is celebrating with wine and TV and song. The whole person needs to take part in the promotion of a mood in conformity with the prayer.

An important element in this is what is called 'colloquy', talking to God and Christ in a familiar way and hearing what they have to say. And Mary too. I need all the help I can get!

When the final week of the *Exercises* is reached, celebrating the resurrection, the mood desired is quite different and welcomes sunshine and flowers.

This approach would appeal to the Celtic soul. They prayed with arms outstretched in the form of a cross, with many genuflections and signs of the cross. And often standing waist-deep in cold seawater! Much of this would be penitential to show their sincerity and single-mindedness; but they had blessings and prayers for all aspects of the day, as we have seen.

There is a breadth of view and attitude in both the Celtic and the Ignatian spirituality which stems from the assumption that God and the Spirit are to be found at work throughout creation. Implicit in the origin of the cosmos with the Big Bang is the knowledge that the whole product of that bang arises from one tiny source which then expands and diversifies into the whole of creation.

However different and diversified the many elements of the universe have become over billions of years there is still a basic common origin of everything. Stemming from this is an assumption that we have more in common with other elements of creation than we have differences.

At the beginning of the *Spiritual Exercises* there is a statement called the Presupposition which is based on this assumption and a consequent respect for the other person and an openness to differences that we may encounter in other peoples' cultures and attitudes. The Presupposition requires that we give every possible space to the other person's opinions and way of thinking. We search for similarities rather than differences. We look abroad for the evidence of the Spirit's work even in situations that are foreign to us and beyond the narrow confines of our own system or beliefs. We seek the truth wherever it can be found, and hence the great interest in learning from the widest possible sources. Teilhard de Chardin's 'cosmic spirituality' covers the planet. 'I consider nothing foreign to me which is human.' (Terence)

It was this attitude, of finding God in all things, and wherever he was found to be at work, that led Ricci in China to dress and act like a Buddhist and de Nobili to become a sanyasi in India and took many of the Celtic monks from Ireland across to the Continent where they established monastic centres of prayer and learning, preserving libraries of manuscripts of the old classical learning. The Jesuit Order has founded many centres of learning, schools and universities across the world.

If we consider, as the Celts did, and as Ignatius did, that God is to be found in all his works, it is not surprising that they found him in the cultures and creativity of the peoples of the earth. In everything God made he lives and works, whistling down the winds of the sea, making the rivers flow, and piping the songbirds' airs. He is in the music of the mountains as he is in the creativity of the human soul. He is still at work creating and shaping the plans that build our cities and even in the crazy twists in the cathedral of Gaudi. He whistles the music into the hearts of a Beethoven and Bach, feeds the words into the creative mind of Hopkins, and into the brilliance of Shakespeare's plots.

No wonder, then, that the uplifted spirit of the Celtic heart should find him at play in every corner of the universe, and in the cultures of the inhabitants of the earth. No wonder that Ignatius would search for him in the learning of the different cultures of the world as well as in the stars, and the Celtic monks would find him in the learning of the ancient Greeks. Jesus said to the woman at the well: 'The hour is coming when you will worship the Father neither on this mountain nor in Jerusalem … but in spirit and in truth.' That truth is to be sought and found in the whole of creation.

> I hear His footsteps in the church's aisles,
> I see his shadow on the city walls,
> I hear his voice that preaches words of truth
> from pulpit or inspired
> Shakespearean lines.
> All creativity arises from His hand
> and learning and all culture
> is from Him
> Who made all things.

CHAPTER EIGHT

Journeying on God's Breath

We stole away because we wanted
For the love of God
To be on pilgrimage,
We cared not where.

These words were given as an explanation to King Alfred of Wessex as to why three Irish men had landed up on the coast of Cornwall after drifting across the sea for seven days in a curragh made of hides, with no oars and few provisions. It represents one of the strangest phenomena of the Celtic Christian Church. Many holy people leapt like lemmings into curraghs and headed off, some with a definite direction, others just letting the wind take them, like the three men above, to wherever the Lord wanted them to go. It is called *peregrinatio* meaning, literally, journeying. Those who thus journeyed were called *peregrini*. Most of them are unknown to us, others are famous, like Brendan the Navigator, and Columba who drifted his way from the north of Ireland to Iona. I was lucky some years ago, to have the opportunity of visiting a remarkable site out in the ocean off the coast of Kerry. It is a huge inaccessible rock standing up out of the sea, defying the onslaught of the waves and weather. It is called Skellig Michael, and it is inaccessible to the extent that only in moments when the sea is kind enough can a landing be made. A group of monks landed there sometime circa AD 500 and built, marvellous to relate, a monastery at the top of this huge rock, complete with chapel, beehive cells, and terraces on which they grew a meagre crop of vegetables to supplement their diet of sea-birds' eggs and flesh. A more extraordinary site for a monastery you could scarcely imagine, perched as it was about 500 metres above the raging sea.

Why would they have done such a thing? Many boatloads of Celts took to the seas, often without a planned direction, letting the wind, the breath of God, send them wherever it would. That destination was, presumably, where God wanted them to be.

There are several possibilities to explain their strange behaviour. One is penance. This might be imposed on the sinner by him or herself or by the Church. Columba may have sailed away from Ireland as a penance perhaps set by himself out of guilt for his involvement in a war with another tribe. He may have been sentenced to it by a court for his having secretly stolen or copied a document of his tutor, Finian (an early case of breaking copyright). A more accessible explanation is connected with the influence of the Egyptian desert on the Christians in Ireland. Strange as it may seem, there was a strong connection between Egypt and Ireland at this time. You may well wonder how there could be such a connection until you realise that there were trade routes across the seas from east to west. Eastern artifacts have been found in Ireland and some of the High Crosses carry a carved reference to a meeting between Paul and Antony in the desert (not the Paul of the epistles). There seems to have been an exchange of monks from east to west, since there is evidence of Egyptian monks buried in Ireland. The influence of the desert fathers and mothers was such that the Celtic Christians wanted to emulate the monks of the desert in their ascetic lifestyle. But alas there is no desert in Ireland. So they used the sea as their desert and travelled to isolated and fierce landscapes in which to express their love of God in their monastic rituals.

Another area in which the Celtic Church exercised considerable creativity was in the matter of martyrdom. Christianity entered Ireland smoothly without the call to martyrdom and the spilling of blood. There were one or two exceptions, as in the case of the monks on the island of Eigg who were burned to death in their monastery by a Pictish queen. But in general there was no call for martyrs to shed their blood. This seemed a great loss to the Celts since they knew what an influence the martyrs in the early Church had on the strengthening of the faith of the Christians. So they invented three sorts of martyrdom: Red, White, and Green, red referring to the sacrificing of one's life for the faith, white referring to the going into exile willingly for the faith, as a sort of sacrificing of life, and green being the leading of life at home (because of commitment to family) but with an ascetic orientation to it.

The white martyrdom was the one with particular reference to *peregrinatio*. Columba, for instance, left home and homeland which he loved, and travelled along the sea road to the west of

Scotland, stopping every now and then to see if Ireland were still visible, and if he could see it he went on, until, on Iona he no longer could see his homeland, and stopped there. He vowed that he would not revisit his home again. Actually he did, but went with a blindfold on!

Would any of the Celts find any rapport in the *Spiritual Exercises* of St Ignatius for their desire for peregrination? Perhaps the two spiritualities come closest together in their desire for doing great deeds.

On his bed of recovery from the wounds of Pamplona Ignatius found himself caught up into the actions of the saints, especially Francis of Assisi and Dominic. He had a great desire to do great deeds for God, as penance for his past life, and as a way of showing God that he was in earnest about his new life. He wanted to emulate the saints in his deeds and penances. It was as though he wanted to impress God by the extreme rigour of his asceticism and so 'buy' God's forgiveness and help. A naïve spirituality indeed, but one which led him deeper into the arms of God.

The Celts were a hero society. Their culture was full of the deeds of heroes which were recounted at their great feasts. When they came to showing God the sincerity of their new faith, they would want it to be in the most total and exemplary way. Only the best, the toughest, the most outlandish action was good enough for God. So they went in their curraghs out to remote places to set up their cells or monasteries where they worshipped God praying with their arms outstretched in the form of a cross, with many genuflections and signs of the cross, and sometimes standing up to the waist in cold seawater.

In a time of crisis in his spiritual testing time at Manresa, Ignatius used to pray for seven hours at a stretch hoping that the severity of his exercise might solve his spiritual problems. Instead it led him to the brink of suicide. But that desire to do great deeds for God has always been embedded in Christianity.

This corresponds to what Bonhoeffer calls 'costly grace'. The call of Christ is not to be had 'on the cheap'. It costs, it demands. And it requires an initial step or response on the part of the one called. When Jesus called Levi to follow him Levi at once got up, left the tax-collector's desk (and his lucrative job) and followed.

God gave his only Son for our sake and the Son gave his life to save us. It was costly for God and our answer to the call of Christ will also be demanding. Ignatius gave his life totally to the following of Christ, and demanded that his followers do the same.

It is this need to do the great, the costly thing that inspired the Celts to undertake the hazardous journeys on the desert of the sea to arrive at remote and demanding scenes where they lived out their lives in an ascetical regime of prayer and penance. Ignatius became a pilgrim, in a pilgrim's plain cloak and expending his energy to such an extent that his health was ruined. His (Jesuit) followers did the same, going wherever there was a need, at whatever cost. Once Francis Xavier moved under the banner of Christ he gave his life to travelling to Japan, India and was on his way to China when he died. Pierre Favre wandered all over Europe to proclaim the kingdom of God, walked himself to death, literally, in his desire to do all he could for God and Christ. The early Jesuits were once described as people 'with one foot in the air' because they were constantly on the move and globetrotting. They discovered how to travel on foot from the north of India through to China, discovering Tibet on the way.

It is really a matter of commitment. The *Spiritual Exercises* are a scheme of prayer and reflection that form the first step in a movement towards a total commitment to the following of Christ into the work of the kingdom. The call itself is individual and from Christ but that first step, the doing of the *Exercises*, is within the choice of the person, just as the first step for Peter – leaving his nets on the shore – was within his own capability and choice. But the call of Christ moves the person to that choice and to all that follows from that choice.

I think that if ever an early Celtic Christian had the opportunity of doing the *Spiritual Exercises* he would recognise it as the sort of call to commitment he knew in *peregrinatio*, putting himself with total trust into the hands of God.

He would recognise it as a call to come into a close relationship to Christ and to hear his call to service of the kingdom and love of the children of God. The journeying on the high seas he knew to be a seeking of the 'Place of Resurrection'. In the

Exercises that would translate into a call to follow Christ in whatever way, through his life and death and into resurrection.

There is a very absolute feature of the call of Christ. As we saw, he called Levi to follow, and at once he got up, left all he possessed and went with Jesus. No arguing, no 'buts', no 'what ifs', but simply instant obedience. It is like the lines we already quoted from Hopkins about the 'call' of the Cross:

Hither then, last or first
To hero of Calvary, Christ's feet –
Never ask if meaning it, wanting it, warned of it – men go.
(Gerard Manley Hopkins, *The Wreck of the Deutschland*)

The same instantaneous response came from Peter who left his nets on the shore and followed Christ. Why should this be so? The only reason seems to be that it is Jesus Christ who calls. The call is absolute, a call with the unaccountable authority of Christ through whom the power of heaven speaks, mastering us and drawing us. It is, again in Hopkins' words 'a vein of the gospel proffer, a pressure, a principle, Christ's gift'.

There are many references in the gospel to the hardship of the following of Jesus – it is no easy option. You are warned that following him involves carrying your cross, dying to self, bearing hardship and opposition, being content with the poverty of Christ – yet people followed him and still do. On the other hand, there is very little to say what the benefits might be. When Peter asked 'What's in it for us?' he was told he would sit on a throne in the kingdom judging the tribes of Israel. Not exactly the person in the street's idea of heaven. Nothing of the here and now except following in Christ's footsteps. I suppose it is a feature of all great leaders, that the motive for following is inherent in the charism of the leader him or herself. Jesus called with 'authority': 'No one has spoken like this man, he speaks with authority.' And what authority! It was the authority of the Son of God. When Jesus called, they followed. The disciple simply leaves his nets, burns his boats, leaves his money, and comes. He comes even though he knows it is to a life that is unpredictable, insecure, and leaving behind what he knows and loves. The Celtic *peregrini* left behind country and home, which for them was an enormous loss. In Celtic society, family and tribe were of primary importance; but they did it for a greater gain, a greater security, a greater family. The first step is to leave all and follow. You cannot run the race if you do not get into the starting-blocks. Both the Celts and Ignatius would know that.

A central part of the *Spiritual Exercises* is what is termed 'Election'. It means the use of 'discernment' to find out and follow out what God wants me to do in my life. In fact, most of the *Exercises* are a preparation for this. We have to know, first of all, what 'the will of God' means. God can be said to have a positive will for each one of us, as opposed to a permissive will. God permits things which he would not prefer. What we are seeking in our discernment of God's will is what he wills positively for me, his actual preference for my life. Many things happen to us in our lives without any choice on our part but that is not our concern in seeking the will of God. But with God's positive will for us, what he prefers for us, we are left the freedom of choice. We can do or not do what God prefers for us. What we are seeking in our choice is to find what is more for the glory of God.

If we are to be successful in our discerning the will of God for us, we must first of all be open to the working of the Holy Spirit so that we will do God's will for us once it is known. If we are open to the Spirit, God will surely help us in our decision. We need to pray to know that preference of God for us, pray earnestly to find it. And, most important, we have to be what Ignatius calls 'indifferent'. It is a very special word for him. It does not quite mean what it means in our ordinary usage of the word. When we say in our ordinary speech that we are indifferent to something, it conjures up a sense of coldness and 'couldn't care less' about it. For Ignatius it refers to a state of mind and soul that keeps the alternatives in balance so that I do not opt for one or the other option unless it leads me closer to God.

Can we say that this seeking of the will of God is present in the lives of the Celtic people? They were certainly very reflective and self-knowledge was important to them. Many of the celtic saints had what they called an *Anam Chara* or 'Soul Friend' to whom they would go, often travelling long distances for the privilege, to talk to him or her of their state of soul, as we would go nowadays to a Spiritual Director. No doubt that would involve seeking the will of God in their lives. Many of them chose a monastic life or a hermit existence, finding in that choice the will of God for them. Such choices are individual, and what is right for one is not necessarily right for another.

The Celts who went on a *peregrinatio* expressed a particular form of trust in God such that their committing themselves to the waves of the sea in their curraghs was a form of allowing God to move them wherever he would to what they called their 'Place of Resurrection', that is, a place where they would find Christ and live out their lives. It required a deep trust in God.

Ignatius wanted to travel to the Holy Land and had got a ship's captain to agree to take him free of charge since he had no money. But the captain made the condition that Ignatius should be able to feed himself on the journey. He therefore collected enough food to last him during that time. But then he began to doubt whether he should keep money or food for the journey because it showed a lack of trust in God. And so he dispensed with them and simply begged for what he needed.

There is a wonderful poem by Mary Oliver about Magellan where she expresses the desires of the explorer but which, to me, also expresses something of the ethos of the *peregrinatio* of the Celts. He wanted to go far from home, seeking islands and risking the wildest places rather than spending a comfortable life at home. Let us be heroes or follow great men.

Whether we seek God by tossing ourselves into the arms of the sea and ending up in a remote place, or we seek God's will by intense prayer and spiritual searching, we are all seeking Christ in our lives in faith, hope and love. If we are open to him he will call us into whatever state of life is right for us. 'Seek and you shall find.' As Christians we must place Christ at the centre of our lives.

> If ever my cozening Eden garden,
> my enclosed pleasure-dome so green
> should cease to nourish my soul's yearning
> and something unspellable,
> something invisible yet strong
> should claw at my heart's desire,
> dragging me off across the rolling seas,

seeking new treasure troves
in some Thin Place
where I would find my hidden soul,
my Fountain,
my depth,
My Self
as Jesus in the desert seeking light
saw his path snaking among impenetrable
rocks to a barren, grace-dissolved-in Cross;
if that is to be my life,
if that is to be my call,
let me not tarry. For that
is the treasure in the field,
my Place of Resurrection.